ECO-FRIENDLY
HOUSEPLANTS

Eco-Friendly

Houseplants

*50 indoor plants that purify the air
in homes and offices*

B.C. Wolverton

WEIDENFELD & NICOLSON
LONDON

First published in Great Britain in 1996 by
George Weidenfeld & Nicolson Ltd
The Orion Publishing Group
Orion House
5 Upper St Martin's Lane
London
WC2H 9EA

A catalogue record for this book is available from
the British Library.

ISBN: 0 297 83484 3

Designed by Graham Davis
Illustrations by Colin Newman and Jennie Dooge
Edited by Cathy Meeus
Photography by Phil Starling

*To my wife and best friend, Yvonne, without whose dedication
and unceasing efforts this book would not have been possible;
and to my son, John, who conducted countless hours of plant
tests and whose computer wizardry made a difficult task seem
much simpler, I owe my deep gratitude. For it is their belief in
me and this technology, that sustain my efforts.*

My sincere appreciation to NASA and, in particular,
the John C. Stennis Space Center, for allowing me
to study nature amidst a world of electronics and
rockets. Specifically, I would like to thank my NASA
colleague, Dr Rebecca McCaleb, who toiled with me
for many years, and to Keith Bounds, and the
secretaries and staff of the Environmental Research
Laboratory. A special thank you to the Plants for
Clean Air Council whose support I continue to rely
upon. Thanks also to my editor, Susan Haynes, who
was so supportive and offered encouragement along
the way.

Special thanks to The Van Hage Garden Company,
Great Amwell, Herts., for supplying plants and
facilities for photography. Additional plants
supplied by Europlants UK Ltd., Bellbor, Herts.

Contents

INTRODUCTION   6

1. INDOOR AIR POLLUTION   8

2. THE LIVING BIOSPHERE   14

3. HOW HOUSEPLANTS PURIFY THE AIR   20

4. A GROWER'S GUIDE   30

5. THE PLANTS   38

INDEX   140

GLOSSARY AND BIBLIOGRAPHY   142

"That's one small step for man, one giant leap for mankind."

Astronaut Neil Armstrong, 1969 Moon Landing

INTRODUCTION

As we race toward the new millennium, technological advances are occurring at an astounding rate. We seem to have an unquenchable thirst for the gadgets and technical wizardry that make our lives more productive and pleasurable. At the same time, however, we struggle to preserve our links with nature, and growing plants in our homes and workplaces is widely accepted as a means of retaining this connection with the natural world. The cold, impersonal reality of steel and concrete are softened by the cool, peaceful effect of live foliage. Yet houseplants can do more than enhance the appearance of our surroundings: they can play an integral role in improving the very essence of our lives – the air we breathe.

In order to conserve energy resources, over the past 25 years buildings have been ever more efficiently sealed from the air outside. While tightly sealed buildings reduce energy consumption, gases from synthetic materials are trapped inside with deleterious effects upon the well-being of their occupants. Many people spend up to 90 per cent of their time indoors, and long-term exposure to these chemical vapours has brought dramatic increases in the number of cases of allergy, asthma, chemical hypersensitivity and cancer.

Indoor air pollution is now considered by many experts to be one of the major threats to health. Attempts to reduce the incidence of "sick building syndrome" have resulted in increased ventilation, the use of low-emission building materials and furnishings, and better preventive maintenance procedures. However, problems still persist. Ironically, the technology arising from futuristic space exploration may have revealed natural solutions that are as old as the earth itself.

The National Aeronautics and Space Administration (NASA), faced with the task of creating a life-support system for planned moon bases, began extensive studies on treating and recycling air and wastewater. These studies led NASA scientists to ask a very important question. How does the earth produce and sustain clean air? The answer, of course, is through the living processes of plants. With this basic knowledge, NASA scientists began to study the development of sustainable, closed ecological life-support facilities. Working towards these goals, scientists at NASA's John C. Stennis Space Center in southern Mississippi discovered that houseplants could purify and revitalize air in sealed test-chambers. This research and later studies co-sponsored by the Plants for Clean Air Council and Wolverton Environmental Services, Inc. are helping to bring about today's "green revolution". As ever-increasing numbers of the population become concerned about the direct correlation between the indoor environment and their health, the

"green revolution" will continue to spread.

Eco-Friendly Houseplants is the culmination of more than 25 years of research. It attempts to stress the importance of indoor air quality and to relate how our existence is interwoven into a symbiotic – or mutually beneficial – relationship with the animals and plants of our living world. Evidence is offered to show how houseplants can indeed become an integral component of healthy buildings, whether homes or offices, and information is provided on how different houseplants can improve the air in one's "personal breathing zone". Fifty houseplants are described, ordered in accordance with an overall rating based on its ability to remove chemical vapours, ease of cultivation, susceptibility to insect infestation, and transpiration (humidification) rate. In addition, details are given of each plant's preferred growing conditions (light levels and temperature), its place of origin, and the best methods for growth and maintenance. With this wealth of practical information and advice, it is hoped that every reader will be able to benefit from *Eco-Friendly Houseplants*.

I

INDOOR AIR POLLUTION

"I durst not laugh for fear of opening my lips and receiving the bad air."

Julius Caesar, William Shakespeare

We are used to thinking of the indoor environment as a safe haven from the evils of air pollution. During "smog alerts" people are generally advised to stay indoors. Yet modern scientific research indicates that the indoor environment may be as much as ten times more polluted than the outdoor environment. In the early 1950s Dr T. G. Randolph became one of the first medical doctors to associate indoor air pollution with allergies and other chronic illnesses. The US Environmental Protection Agency (EPA) currently ranks indoor air pollution as one of the top five threats to public health. Yet millions of people fail to realize the serious nature of the problem, or even worse, fail to recognize that there is a problem. Today, people living in industrialized societies spend as much as 90 per cent of their lives indoors. Increased exposure to indoor air pollutants in the community directly correlates to an increase in the number and severity of allergic reactions.

THE IMPACT OF THE ENERGY CRISIS

In the United States indoor air quality (IAQ) problems became widespread soon after the 1973–4 energy crisis. In 1973 the Organization of Petroleum Exporting Countries (OPEC) declared an oil embargo against the industrialized nations. In an effort to maximize energy efficiency and to help reduce spiralling energy costs, the building industry began to seal buildings hermetically and to reduce fresh air exchanges. In the United States everyone was encouraged to insulate their homes. The Internal Revenue Service even offered substantial tax incentives to homeowners who installed additional insulation to reduce fuel consumption for heating and air-conditioning. Most people dutifully added extra insulation in the walls and ceilings and applied mastic or weather-stripping to exclude outside air.

CONTROLLING VENTILATION AND HUMIDITY

Ventilation helps to control indoor air pollution by diluting stale indoor air with fresh outside air. Of course, a presumption is made that the outside air is clean, which may not be the case. Certain levels of ventilation are necessary to provide human comfort. Additional ventilation is needed to remove moisture, heat and odours. It remains a balancing act to provide sufficient ventilation for comfort, without necessitating excessive energy consumption.

Respiratory infections are a well-known consequence of poorly maintained air-conditioning systems. Maintenance of such systems is an important factor in ensuring good air quality. In the home, air filters, when regularly replaced, can help to clean outside air as it enters the building. In large buildings IAQ problems are commonly associated with cooling towers, the placement of air-intake vents and poor maintenance of mechanical systems, air ducts, and so on. The *Legionella* bacterium, the cause of legionnaire's disease, has been identified in cooling towers and other stagnant water reservoirs.

Low relative-humidity levels are also associated with poor IAQ. Healthy humidity levels range between 35 and 65 per cent. Often, especially in winter months, humidity drops well below the ideal range. Cold winter air is normally dry. When heating systems are in operation, the air becomes even drier. Dry, arid conditions irritate sensitive membranes in the nose, increasing susceptibility to assaults by airborne chemicals, viruses and allergens. Frequent colds, allergic attacks and asthma during winter months are often caused by low relative humidity.

Humidity levels in excess of 70 per cent can also result in IAQ problems. Humidity in this range may cause mould and mildew damage to furniture and electronic equipment and may create health problems for building occupants. Central-heating and air-conditioning systems can combat high humidity by stripping moisture from the air. However, they cannot add moisture when the humidity level drops below the optimum range.

EMISSIONS FROM MODERN MATERIALS

In recent decades, a subtle change in the composition of building materials and furnishings has been taking place. Pressed wood products or fibreboard often replace natural wood in building construction; wall-to-wall carpeting is ever more common; furnishings in the home and office are no longer made mostly of natural materials, but are composed of synthetics that are held together with a variety of glues and resins. A

Sources of chemical emissions

	Formaldehyde	Xylene/toluene	Benzene	Trichloroethylene	Chloroform	Ammonia	Alcohols	Acetone
Adhesives	■	■	■				■	
Bioeffluents		■				■	■	■
Blueprint machines						■		
Carpeting							■	
Caulking or mastic compounds	■	■	■				■	
Ceiling tiles	■	■	■				■	
Chlorinated tap water					■			
Cleaning products						■		
Computer VDU screens		■						
Cosmetics							■	■
Duplicating machines				■				
Electrophotographic printers		■	■	■		■		
Draperies	■							
Fabrics	■							
Facial tissues	■							
Floor coverings	■	■	■				■	
Gas cookers	■							
Grocery bags	■							
Microfiche developers						■		
Nail polish remover								■
Office correction fluid								■
Paints	■	■	■				■	
Paper towels	■							
Particleboard or chipboard	■	■	■				■	
Permanent-press clothing	■							
Photocopiers		■	■	■		■		
Plywood			■					
Pre-printed paper forms								■
Stains and varnishes	■	■	■				■	
Tobacco smoke			■					
Upholstery	■							
Wall coverings		■	■				■	

plethora of electronic devices for our comfort, work or pleasure are found in our homes, offices and public buildings. These devices are known to emit various organic compounds.

Synthetic materials release hundreds of volatile organic chemicals (VOCs) into the air.

Some common emissions and their sources are listed in the table above.

Humans are also a source of pollution, especially when living or working in closed, poorly ventilated areas. This becomes very apparent when a large number of people are present in a confined space for an extended period of time such as on an airplane journey. Over a period of many years Russian and American space scientists established that, in addition to carbon dioxide, we release as many as 150 volatile substances into the atmosphere, such as carbon monoxide, hydrogen, methane, alcohols, phenols, methyl indole, aldehydes, ammonia, hydrogen sulphide, volatile fatty acids, indol, mercaptans and nitrogen oxides (dioxide). Substances emitted through normal biological processes are termed bioeffluents. Studies have been conducted to determine the rate of bioeffluent emissions for each person. They have shown that acetone, ethyl alcohol, methyl alcohol and ethyl acetate are the principal bioeffluents emitted.

To sum up, the three primary sources of poor indoor air quality are: hermetically sealed buildings and their synthetic furnishings, reduced ventilation, and human bioeffluents. The lack of foresight by architects, engineers and health officials in predicting the consequences of modern building design for the quality of the air we breathe has brought us to the brink of a modern-day health disaster.

HEALTH AND INDOOR AIR POLLUTION

During the early 1980s a number of illnesses began to appear in Europe, Canada and the United States where buildings have been hermetically sealed for energy-efficiency. Since that time, indoor air pollution has become widespread and a phenomenon known as "sick building syndrome" (SBS) has been added to our vocabulary. SBS is a term sometimes used

Symptoms associated with sick building syndrome

- Allergies
- Asthma
- Eye, nose and throat irritations
- Fatigue
- Headache
- Nervous-system disorders
- Respiratory congestion
- Sinus congestion

to describe a collection of symptoms experienced by a high proportion of those living or working in a particular building or part of a building. While standard analysis can detect no cause or origin for their illness, when the building occupants are away for a given time, the symptoms usually diminish, only to recur upon re-entry into the building. Some common symptoms associated with SBS are listed in the panel above left.

The term building-related illness (BRI) is used to describe diseases that can be identified with specific causes. Examples of BRI include lung cancer from asbestos exposure and legionnaire's disease caused by bacteria in stagnant water in air-conditioning or heating systems.

In 1984 a World Health Organization report suggested that as many as 30 per cent of new and remodelled buildings worldwide may have indoor air quality problems. In August 1989 the EPA submitted a report to the US Congress on the quality of indoor air found in ten energy-efficient public buildings. Some chemical concentrations were 100 times greater than normal background levels. This report stated that "sufficient evidence exists to conclude that indoor air pollution represents a major portion of the public's exposure to air pollution and may pose serious acute and chronic health risk." Indoor air pollution may pose an even greater threat than outdoor pollution – primarily because of the greater length of exposure.

According to a report from the Institute of Medicine entitled *Indoor Allergens: Assessing and*

Controlling Adverse Health Effects, one in five Americans will experience allergy-related illness at some point during their lives, and indoor allergens will be responsible for a substantial number of those cases. The report describes allergy as "the state of immune hypersensitivity that exists in an individual who has been exposed to an allergen and has responded with an overproduction of certain immune system components such as immunoglobulin E (IgE) antibodies. About 40 per cent of the population have IgE antibodies against environmental allergens, 20 per cent have clinical allergic disease and 10 per cent have significant or severe allergic disease."

Dr T. G. Randolph is credited with founding the medical discipline known as clinical ecology. Many clinical ecologists are specialists in allergic disorders, who began to split off from their colleagues in the 1950s, arguing that environmental toxins can be as deleterious to health as infectious microorganisms. Many physicians continue to label patients suffering from MCS as having psychiatric disorders. The massive volumes of scientific data emerging from thousands of cases of MCS and SBS are providing overwhelming evidence that Dr Randolph's analysis was correct.

HIGH-RISK GROUPS

Susceptibility to allergens and pollutants varies significantly between individuals. Reactions can range from no observable effects to sneezing, asthma, lung and other respiratory irritations, and even to cancer. Most customers who enter fabric, furniture or carpeting stores can smell formaldehyde and VOCs. Many experience burning eyes and throat or have other respiratory irritations. Contact-lens wearers often experience severe eye irritation.

Illnesses caused by synthetic contaminants in indoor air are most often the result of exposure to low concentrations of a mixture of chemicals. Those exposed to this chemical soup may not immediately experience acute reactions. However, when exposed over an extended period, they may become sensitized. The condition of hypersensitivity is termed "multiple chemical sensitivity" (MCS). Once a person has become hypersensitive, he or she may later develop acute reactions when again exposed to even trace levels of chemical or other pollutants. A hypersensitive individual may also exhibit increased allergic reactions to a wide range of other substances, such as dust, house-dust mites, mould spores, pollen and certain foods. Infants and small children are especially susceptible to indoor air pollution. In approximately 90 per cent of children with asthma, the disease is allergic in nature. This suggests that contaminants in the indoor environment, including tobacco smoke, may have initially damaged sensitive membranes surrounding the airways in the lungs.

Indoor air pollution could also be a major factor in sudden infant death syndrome (SIDS). SIDS, or cot death, is the sudden unexpected death due to unknown causes of infants between the ages of two weeks and one year. Most cases of SIDS occur between two and four months of age. Various neurophysio-logical, immunological and other disturbances have been suggested to explain the occurrence of SIDS. Interestingly, studies have found SIDS is more frequent during cold months, when air pollution problems are also more prevalent. One possible explanation for SIDS is that babies become sensitized to synthetic chemicals even before birth. Foetuses are exposed to the same pollutants as their mothers, but their dynamic growth state makes them more vulnerable to the adverse effects of such exposure. SIDS has also been linked to exposure to tobacco smoke.

Most newborn babies come home from hospital to a freshly painted nursery, complete with new carpeting, cot, mattresses, blankets, clothing and toys, in other words, a room that is likely to be high in chemical emissions. Hopefully, further research will one day produce the definitive answer for the cause of SIDS. Meanwhile, it can be said that babies are exposed to a barrage of indoor contaminants and exposure is unhealthy, if not fatal. Wherever possible, avoid exposing a young baby to new products made of synthetic materials unless the products are first washed several times or allowed to air outdoors.

There are currently hundreds of cases of litigation linked to SBS wending their way through the US courts. The types of buildings involved include schools, courthouses, office buildings, hospitals and nursing homes. One in five American children is said to attend a school with poor indoor air quality.

Carpeting is one of the major sources of indoor air pollution. Although newly installed carpeting produces the most complaints from emissions of irritating chemicals, older carpets harbour dust, house-dust mites, microbes and particulate matter. Carpet, through normal wear and tear, begins to break down over time. Minute carpet fibres become airborne, especially during vacuuming, creating dust which can act as a carrier for microbes. Most carpets and rugs are made of synthetic fibres bound to a backing material by glues and other bonding agents. Research suggests the main culprit may come from a commonly used latex substance called styrene butadiene rubber (SBR).

LOOKING TO THE FUTURE

Perhaps this is a good time for a reality check. We all enjoy the comforts and conveniences of living in the age of technical wizardry. At the same time, however, we must take reasonable measures to protect our health and well-being. We are all told to take precautions against the harmful ultraviolet rays of the sun. We should also be mindful of the need to protect ourselves from the harmful effects of pollutants.

Most experts now agree that indoor air pollution is a major problem. There is no agreement, however, on how to solve it. Increasing the levels of ventilation does not offer a solution to the problem. Constant purging of air inside a building is neither cost-effective nor environmentally responsible.

Although the term "green building" is becoming an attractive concept to building managers and building occupants, the use of living plants is not currently part of the concept. The building industry has instituted a programme of source management – that is, the practice of allowing building materials and furnishings to "off-gas" before they are placed in a building. Building managers are more diligently monitoring mechanical components to ensure their cleanliness and operational efficiency. Architects and engineers are beginning to design buildings using carpets, paints and furniture with lower emissions, and are working to ensure movement of air throughout buildings. Homeowners should also regularly provide preventive maintenance for mechanical systems. They, too, should allow new furnishings to off-gas before bringing them into the home. A further step should include the design of houseplants into each building to help provide an environment that mimics the way that nature cleans the earth's atmosphere.

2

In the beginning God created the heaven and the earth.

Genesis 1:1

THE LIVING BIOSPHERE

The best scientific evidence available indicates that the earth is approximately 4.5 billion years old and that the first forms of life on earth were microorganisms. Millions of years after the appearance of microbes, plants appeared on earth. It is important to note that before plants could survive, microorganisms had to be established in the earth's soil and water. Microorganisms are essential to plants because they convert organic and inorganic substances into a form that can be used by plants for their food. It was many millions of years after plants were established that higher forms of life first appeared. The zone on earth in which life naturally occurs extends from the deep crust to the lower atmosphere, and is commonly referred to as the biosphere. Plants were an essential component of the evolutionary processes that converted the earth from a highly toxic environment into the living, self-regulating system it is today.

In its simplest form, the earth can be viewed as a living organism. Rainforests act as the earth's lungs, producing oxygen and removing carbon dioxide – the opposite process to human and animal lungs. Wetlands function as the earth's kidneys. Aquatic plants filter nutrients and environmental toxins from the water as it flows back into streams, rivers and oceans in much the same way as kidneys filter impurities from our blood.

Evolutionary processes over billions of years converted the earth into a dynamic planet in which each living component (microbes, plants and animals) exists in a harmonious relationship with other life forms. Oxygen produced during photosynthesis – the process by which green plants use light to convert carbon dioxide and water for energy – is vital to all organisms that require oxygen for respiration. The living processes of animals would deplete the atmosphere of oxygen if it were not replenished by photosynthesis. Life-supporting oxygen is produced by plants and carried over the earth's entire surface by wind currents. The wide diversity of plant life distributed throughout the world influences the creation of many micro-climatic zones. Geography, biology and human intervention are all factors that greatly determine local environmental and climatic conditions. For instance, the removal of trees and other vegetation from vast areas of land causes environmental changes in soil composition and weather patterns.

Plants supply many human needs through their use as food, in medicines, for energy, and as building materials, etc. Edible plants provide essential nourishment for many living creatures. Certain plants contain chemicals that are useful as medicines. Others are valuable for their fibres, such as cotton, flax and hemp. Fossil fuels, a major energy source, are derived from plants. There are approximately 400,000 plant species on earth. The greatest number of species are found in the tropical regions surrounding the equator.

Photosynthesis in plants is not only essential for the maintenance of all higher forms of life, but is also a process of immense magnitude. An estimated 170 billion tons of dry plant biomass is produced through photosynthesis by all plants on earth each year. For every dry ton of new plant biomass produced through photosynthesis, approximately 1,273 kg (1.4 tons) of oxygen are added to the atmosphere and approximately 1,636 kg (1.8 tons) of carbon dioxide are removed. Studies conducted by the US and Russian space agencies show that astronauts consume approximately 0.9 kg (2 lb) of oxygen and exhale approximately 1.1 kg (2.4 lb) of carbon dioxide every 24 hours. Based on this data, approximately 0.64 kg (1.4 lb) of new dry plant material must be produced by photosynthesis each day to supply the oxygen needs of one adult.

A CLOSER LOOK

Close study reveals that individual plants create their own mini-ecosystem. From large trees to houseplants originating underneath the canopy of dense forests, each plant creates a micro-environment around its leaves and roots. Activity taking place within this micro-environment enables the plant to survive and grow. To the human eye, plants may appear static and non-reactive as they continue their normal process of living and growing. But in scientific terms, plants are highly dynamic, actively creating and emitting a cloud of complex, invisible substances around their leaves and roots that provide for their protection and well-being. The area of soil near plant roots is filled with biological activity. This area, known as the rhizosphere, is influenced by substances excreted by plant roots. The rhizosphere is itself an active ecosystem in which populations of microorganisms are generally much greater than in soil further from the roots. Each plant excretes a complex mixture of sugars, amino acids, hormones, organic acids and other substances that stimulate the growth of specific microbes it needs for survival, and inhibit microbes that would be harmful. The type and number of microbes maintained by plant roots differ from plant to plant depending upon its geographical location. Scientists know less about the substances emitted by plant leaves. These substances appear to have beneficial functions, such as controlling humidity levels and protecting the plant from invasion by insects and airborne microbes.

PHOTOSYNTHESIS

An understanding of the basic processes involved in plant growth and survival aids us in the care and nurturing of our houseplants. Like all living beings, plants use sugar for energy. Plants differ from other living organisms in that they have the unique ability to manufacture their own sugar through the process of photosynthesis. Photosynthesis takes place only in the presence of light.

Plants absorb carbon dioxide from the atmosphere through tiny openings in the leaves called stomata. Plant roots absorb moisture from the soil. Chlorophyll and other green tissues in the leaves absorb radiant energy from a light source. This energy is used to split water molecules into oxygen and hydrogen. Through complex chemical reactions, plants use hydrogen and carbon dioxide to form sugars. Oxygen, a by-product of photosynthesis, is released into the atmosphere.

Sugars produced by photosynthesis not only provide food for the plant but also serve as a source of energy that is used to synthesize other chemicals required for life, and thus, add a vast amount of energy to the biosphere. The life processes of all organisms require continual expenditure of energy. Without this source of energy, life on this planet would soon cease. Furthermore, all of the many organic compounds that are essential constituents of cell structures are derived ultimately from sugars or other organic compounds produced by plants through photosynthesis.

RESPIRATION

Respiration is the process by which food (sugars) combines with oxygen and biologically "burns" to release energy and heat. Respiration is fundamentally a chemical process of oxidation or slow combustion. It differs from combustion in that it proceeds slowly without the rapid build-up of excessive heat. During respiration, oxygen and sugars are consumed (oxidized) to produce energy for the manufacture of other substances required for growth and survival. Carbon dioxide and water are by-products of respiration and are released into the atmosphere, as is excess heat that may result from the process.

TRANSPIRATION

Evaporation of water from plant leaves is called transpiration. The combination of evaporation from soil and transpiration from plant leaves is called evapotranspiration. Waxy cuticles on leaf surfaces restrict diffusion so that most water vapour, oxygen, and other gases must pass

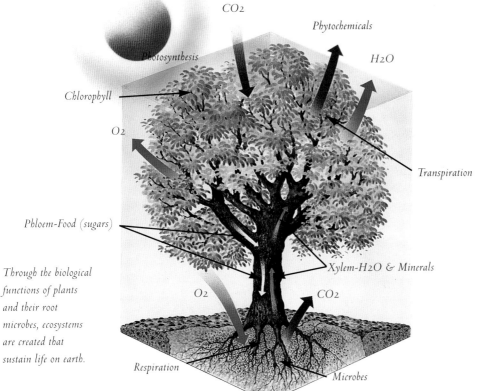

CO2

Photosynthesis

Phytochemicals

H2O

Chlorophyll

O2

Transpiration

Phloem-Food (sugars)

Xylem-H2O & Minerals

Through the biological functions of plants and their root microbes, ecosystems are created that sustain life on earth.

O2

CO2

Respiration

Microbes

through the stomata. These small openings are usually found on both upper and lower surfaces of leaves, but may sometimes be found only on the undersides. They are surrounded by guard cells which control closing and opening. When plant roots become dry, guard cells close the stomata to prevent further water loss. If plants transpire more water than they can absorb through their roots, they will wilt.

Many changes in environmental factors influence opening and closing of stomata. In most plants stomata open at sunrise and close in darkness. Some plants, including most succulents, orchids and bromeliads, act in an opposite manner, opening their stomata at night. The primary reason for this reversal is to conserve water during hot, sunny days.

The role of transpiration has been discussed for many years by plant physiologists. Air movement may be created during periods of high transpiration. Whenever there is a significant difference between the temperature of leaf surfaces and air, convection currents are created, causing an air flow even when there is no other air movement. This is important for plants that live underneath the dense forest canopy where there is virtually no other form of air movement. Some of these plants, including most plants that we use as houseplants, have unusually high photosynthetic rates. This allows them to thrive in dimly lit forests. Transpiration rates in a great many of these plants are also high. As water moves rapidly from the soil surrounding the roots up through the plant, air is pulled down around roots adding nitrogen gas and oxygen to the soil. Through a biological process called nitrogen fixation, certain microbes can convert atmospheric nitrogen gas into nitrate, a chemical that plants use as a nutrient.

The ability to produce movement of air is important in helping houseplants remove toxins from the indoor environment. Because the conditioned air inside buildings is naturally dry, higher transpiration rates aid the movement of toxin-laden air to the root zone where microbes in the soil can break down the gases into a source of food and energy.

LEAF ABSORPTION AND TRANSLOCATION

Plant leaves not only produce life-sustaining oxygen, but also play a major role in maintaining the health of both the plant and its root microbes. Leaf absorption of carbon dioxide and transport of a variety of chemicals from one part of the plant to other parts are essential to plant function.

The term translocation has been used to describe the movement of substances throughout the plant. Translocation in plants involves two complex tissue systems, xylem and phloem. The primary function of the xylem is to move minerals and water from the roots to plant foliage. Sugars and other dissolved foods move from plant foliage to all non-green cells through the phloem. Xylem and phloem also have secondary, interconnecting paths that allow them to reverse their primary functions under certain conditions.

Research has shown that some organic substances applied to leaves, are translocated not only to the roots, but even into the surrounding soil. The systemic insecticide industry is built around this ability of plants to absorb and translocate chemicals.

Organic chemicals that are translocated from the atmosphere to the rhizosphere (root zone) undoubtedly influence the types and numbers of microorganisms in the soil surrounding the plant. This has important implications in demonstrating the potential of houseplant leaves to absorb volatile organic chemicals (VOCs) from indoor air and translocate these chemicals unchanged to root areas where they are broken down by microbes. Some organic chemicals absorbed by plants from the atmosphere are destroyed by the plant's own biological processes, without involving the action of microbes in the soil.

SUBSTANCES RELEASED BY PLANT LEAVES

Plants emit many different substances into the air surrounding their leaves. The most studied and understood substance is water vapour. Plants play an important role in controlling humidity levels and climatic conditions. The amount of water vapour in the air is called humidity. The relative humidity is the amount of water in the air compared to the maximum amount the air could hold at that temperature. For example, a relative humidity of 50 per cent means that the air contains half the amount of moisture it can hold before becoming saturated or reaching its dew point. As moist warm air rises, it slowly cools until its relative humidity reaches 100 per cent. At this saturation point, clouds form and, under certain conditions, the moisture falls to earth as precipitation.

Volatile chemicals released by plant leaves appear to be an important factor in controlling airborne microbes and mould spores in the surrounding air.

ROOT MICROBES

A varied population of microorganisms live in the soil. They are responsible for making nutrients available to plants, releasing soil minerals, breaking down organic waste materials and detoxifying many environmental poisons that reach the soil. Their work is vital for soil fertility and plant growth. However, not all soil microorganisms are beneficial to plants. Some may cause plant disease or even compete with plants for nutrients.

The zone of soil influenced by plant roots, the rhizosphere, contains more microbes than other soil because of the availability of food. Many organic compounds excreted from the roots or dead root cells serve as a food source for microbes. Plant scientists have gathered extensive research data over the past 50 years to show how substances excreted by plant roots exert a distinct selective action on microbes, resulting in stimulation of certain groups, while suppressing others. It appears that each plant is equipped by nature with its own genetic codes. These codes determine the types and numbers of microbes needed for the plant to survive.

Microbes assist in several ways to help maintain the health and well-being of their host plant. They function as guards by repelling other microbes that could harm plants. Microbes digest fallen leaves and other debris found near plant roots, producing food for the plant. Substances secreted by plant roots stimulate rapid multiplication, death and decay of microbial cells. These decaying microbial cells also serve as a source of food for plants.

Microbes are highly adaptive organisms, having the ability to mutate over relatively short periods of time to cope with changes in the environment. In particular, certain bacteria commonly found in the rhizosphere of some plants have been observed to adapt to be able to break down a variety of environment pollutants. It is therefore clear that the co-operative relationship between plants and microbes is not only important for plant survival but also serves a vital function in creating a healthy environment for man and other living creatures.

PHYTOCHEMICALS

The chemicals that plants manufacture are called phytochemicals. Phytochemicals are produced in leaves or secreted by plant roots. They reduce competition from other plants or protect them from microbes, insects and animals. For example, some plants produce terpenes (volatile substances) that inhibit germination or root growth of other plants.

Many of our most important medicines originate from the phytochemicals of plants. Some familiar examples are: aspirin, derived from willow bark; quinine, used for the treatment of malaria, from cinchona bark; digitalis, a heart stimulant, from dried leaves of the purple foxglove (*Digitalis purpurea*); and taxol, from the Pacific yew tree (*Taxus brevifolia*), a promising new drug used in the treatment of cancer. Indeed, hundreds of important medicines now in use are plant derivatives. The screening of plants for new pharmaceuticals is still in its infancy. One of the fastest growing fields of medicine and nutrition today is the rediscovery of the many beneficial uses of herbs, phytochemicals and other plant products. We risk our supply of these valuable chemicals each time a species becomes extinct. In fact, we put our very health at risk with the destruction of forests around the world.

Whether one views the earth from outer space or the micro-environment of a single plant, a dynamic state of activity is taking place. Many of the symbiotic relationships that drive this planet are also taking place on a microscopic scale. Complex interactions like photosynthesis, microbial activity, transpiration and translocation play important roles in making this the only planet in the universe known to support life. All forms of life weave an intricate web of dependency upon one another, and humans, as guardians of the earth, must balance these life processes with our technological advances to ensure the sustainability of the living biosphere.

3

"The highest mission of plants is not merely to please our eyes with color, our mouths with delicious fruits. Not only do they do this and more, but they are ever silently but surely eating up what is impure and injurious to ourselves in the atmosphere and in the earth all around our homes; and any dwelling in which plants are well and healthily grown will be more likely to be a clean and healthy house than if plants were not there."

Attributed to the Ladies' Floral Cabinet, *19th century*

HOW HOUSEPLANTS
PURIFY THE AIR

Science is now catching up with what gardeners have known for decades: that by growing plants we can relieve stress, while helping to clean the environment. A growing body of research shows that cultivating plants indoors and outdoors may be the best medicine available for improving mental and physical well-being at any age. Studies of interactions between plants and people have provided overwhelming evidence that plants have a measurable beneficial effect on people and the spaces they inhabit. Gardening in general has become one of the most popular leisure activities, and the cultivation of houseplants in particular has developed an enthusiastic following.

Plants not only add beauty to a room, but also make it a friendly, inviting place to live or work: they appear to have a calming, spiritual effect on most people. This perhaps explains why plants play such an important role at key stages in our lives, such as weddings, funerals, periods of illness, and birthdays. People feel relaxed when they are near or tending to living plants. Businesses install interior landscaping to increase worker-productivity and reduce absenteeism. Top hotels, restaurants, and other commercial premises use plants to help attract customers.

NASA PLANT STUDIES

As plans for a manned moonbase were developed, NASA scientists began to study the feasibility of a closed ecological life-support system. Skylab missions revealed additional problems facing inhabitants of a closed facility. Analyses of the air inside spacecraft proved that air quality would be a major concern. Monitoring by a highly sensitive gas chromatograph coupled with a mass spectrometer detected the presence of more than 300 volatile organic chemicals (VOCs) in the air inside the spacecraft during occupancy by its crew.

In 1980 NASA's John C. Stennis Space Center first discovered that houseplants could remove VOCs from sealed test chambers. NASA's studies, published in 1984, demonstrated the ability of plants to remove formaldehyde from test chambers. These findings were enthusiastically received by the public and, in particular, by interior plantscapers and houseplant growers. Realizing the potential value of this research, the Associated Landscape Contractors of America (ALCA) jointly funded a two-year study with NASA to further evaluate the ability of 12 common houseplants to remove formaldehyde, benzene and trichloroethylene from sealed chambers. As a consequence of the positive results from this study, published in late 1989, ALCA created the Plants for Clean Air Council (PCAC), a non-profit organization, that

continues to support the cultivation of plants as a method of improving indoor air quality.

NASA's "BIOHOME"

As with any new discovery, there were some critics of the research. The most vocal critics complained that sealed-chamber studies could not be extrapolated into "real-world" environments. To address these and other relevant concerns, NASA developed a small, tightly sealed structure called the "Biohome".

The Biohome, with its futuristic design, was engineered to achieve maximum air and energy insulation. Because the interior was constructed of plastic and other synthetic materials, the emission of many VOCs was anticipated. People entering the Biohome experienced typical symptoms associated with sick building syndrome, such as burning eyes and throat, and breathing problems.

Air samples were taken before and after the addition of indoor plants and an activated-carbon plant filter. This fan-assisted planter had the VOC removal capacity of approximately 15 houseplants. Six large philodendrons and one fan-assisted activated-carbon planter containing golden pothos were placed inside the Biohome. After several days, air samples were again analysed and showed substantial reduction of VOCs. Chemical analyses of VOC removal were important for scientific validation. However, the ultimate proof was exhibited by the fact that individuals who entered the Biohome no longer experienced symptoms associated with sick building syndrome. The Biohome study provided proof that plants can become an integral component in maintaining healthy air inside hermetically sealed buildings.

Upon completion of these studies, a

Exterior view of NASA Biohome.

Air purification and wastewater treatment system in Biohome.

Courtesy of the National Aeronautics and Space Administration.

Dining and entertainment area of Biohome.

student lived in the Biohome during the summer of 1989 and had no complaints about indoor air quality. Interior plants were successfully used to alleviate sick building syndrome in this super energy-efficient structure. In the past, houseplants were sought only for their beauty and psychological value.

The ability of houseplants to improve the quality of the air we breathe is now an accepted scientific fact.

FORMALDEHYDE REMOVAL BY PLANTS

In 1990 PCAC and Wolverton Environmental Services, Inc. began to co-sponsor research that

Removal rates of formaldehyde by houseplants

Plant	µg per hour		Plant	µg per hour
Boston fern	████████████████████		Chinese evergreen	███████
Florist's mum	█████████████████		Spider plant	███████
Gerbera daisy	████████████████		Banana	███████
Dwarf date palm	████████████████		Red emerald philodendron	██████
Janet Craig	████████████████		Dumb cane (Camilla)	█████
Bamboo palm	████████████████		Elephant ear philodendron	█████
Kimberley queen fern	███████████████		Golden pothos	██████
Rubber plant	█████████████		Norfolk Island pine	█████
English ivy	█████████████		Wax begonia	█████
Weeping fig	███████████		Prayer plant	████
Peace lily	██████████		Oak leaf ivy	████
Areca palm	███████████		Christmas cactus	████
Corn plant	██████████		Lacy tree philodendron	████
Lady palm	█████████		Arrowhead vine	████
Schefflera	█████████		Heart-leaf philodendron	████
Dragon tree	████████		Lady Jane	████
Warneckei	████████		Peacock plant	████
Lily turf	████████		Poinsettia	████
Dendrobium orchid	████████		Cyclamen	████
Dumb cane (Exotica)	████████		Moth orchid	███
Tulip	███████		Urn plant	███
Ficus alii	██████		Croton	███
King of hearts	███████		Snake plant	██
Parlour palm	███████		Aloe vera	██
Azalea	██████		Kalanchoe	██

continues to expand upon the earlier NASA research. Fifty houseplants have been tested to date for their ability to remove various toxic gases from sealed test-chambers. Because formaldehyde is the most commonly found toxin in indoor air, the ability to remove this substance from the air was used as the standard for rating these plants. Formaldehyde has provoked more public, regulatory and scientific controversy during the past 15 years than any other substance. Numerous sources of formaldehyde are present in the buildings we inhabit. It is found in various resins and is used to treat many consumer products,

Removal rates of xylene and toluene by houseplants (top 14 tested)

Plant	µg per hour
Areca palm	■■■■■■■■■■■■■■■■■■■
Dwarf date palm	■■■■■■■■■■■■■■■■■
Moth orchid	■■■■■■■■■■■■■■
Dumb cane (Camilla)	■■■■■■■■■■
Dragon tree	■■■■■■■■■
Dendrobium orchid	■■■■■■■■■
Dumb cane (Exotica)	■■■■■■■■■
King of hearts	■■■■■■■■
Kimberley queen fern	■■■■■■■■
Warneckei	■■■■■■■
Lady Jane	■■■■■■
Corn plant	■■■■■■
Weeping fig	■■■■■■
Peace lily	■■■■■■

neuropsychological problems. Although evidence of cancer formation in rodents exposed to formaldehyde is unequivocal, the extrapolation of these results to humans has been controversial.

Comparative removal rates of formaldehyde for all 50 houseplants are shown in the table on page 23. Additional tables (left and below) list the best plants for the removal of certain other chemicals. As additional plants are tested, the best plants for each chemical may change. Because of their similar chemical properties, tests for xylene and toluene were combined. Substances that are known to emit these chemicals are listed in Chapter One.

Many houseplants have been tested for their

including refuse sacks, paper towels, facial tissues, fabrics, permanent-press clothing, carpet-backing, floor-coverings and adhesives. Formaldehyde is released by gas cookers and is found in tobacco smoke. It is also used in building materials such as plywood, chipboard and panelling. Both plywood and chipboard are used extensively in the manufacture of domestic and office furniture and fittings.

Numerous adverse health problems have been ascribed to formaldehyde exposure, ranging from well-documented effects such as eye, nose and throat irritation, to more controversial claims including asthma, cancer, chronic respiratory diseases and

Removal rates of ammonia by houseplants (top 14 tested)

Plant	µg per hour
Lady palm	■■■■■■■■■■■■■■■■■■
King of hearts	■■■■■■■■■■■■■■
Lily turf	■■■■■■■■■■■■
Lady Jane	■■■■■■■■■■
Florist's mum	■■■■■■■■
Peacock plant	■■■■■■■■
Dendrobium orchid	■■■■■■■■
Tulip	■■■■■■■
Parlour palm	■■■■■
Arrowhead vine	■■■■■
Weeping fig	■■■■
Peace lily	■■■■
Corn plant	■■■
Azalea	■■■

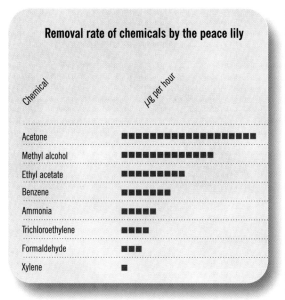

Removal rate of chemicals by the peace lily

Chemical	μg per hour
Acetone	■■■■■■■■■■■■■■■■■■■■
Methyl alcohol	■■■■■■■■■■■■■■
Ethyl acetate	■■■■■■■■■
Benzene	■■■■■■■
Ammonia	■■■■■
Trichloroethylene	■■■■
Formaldehyde	■■■
Xylene	■

ability to remove volatile chemicals. The table above shows the comparative rate of removal of various chemicals by the peace lily.

One concern voiced by those sceptical of these findings centres around the belief that if plants continually absorb toxins from the air, once absorption capacity is reached, the plant will die and release all of the toxins back into the air. To address these concerns, the lady palm's ability to remove formaldehyde released from sections of panelling was tested. Two chambers were used in these experiments. The first chamber held a lady palm and two sections of panelling made from urea-formaldehyde resins. The second (control) chamber held only two sections of panelling and a beaker of water, to help equalize the humidity levels in the two chambers. Plant transpiration naturally increased the humidity in the first chamber.

The lady palm not only removed formaldehyde fumes, but its removal rate improved with exposure time. Interestingly,

there was no apparent damage to the plant. Studies with other chemicals have shown that some houseplants can rapidly increase their ability to remove toxins from sealed chambers after 24-hour exposures. This phenomenon indicates that plants play a major role in delivering airborne toxins to microbes living around their roots, which can then break down the toxin. The adaptation of microbes to this task is the key to houseplants becoming better fighters against air pollution.

Other aspects of indoor air quality

Bioeffluents released during human respiration also increase IAQ problems. Four of the most prevalent bioeffluents found in a crowded classroom are shown in the table below. As can be seen in this chart, houseplants can be very effective in removing bioeffluents from the ambient air.

Bioeffluents and VOCs are not the only contributors to poor indoor air quality. The presence of airborne microbes, such as mould spores, and low relative humidity are also determining factors in the quality of the air.

Bioeffluent removal by the peace lily

Ethyl alcohol	✿✿✿✿✿✿✿✿✿✿✿✿✿✿✿✿✿✿✿✿✿✿
	■
Acetone	✿✿✿✿✿✿✿✿✿✿✿✿✿✿✿✿✿
	■
Methyl alcohol	✿✿✿✿✿✿✿
	■■
Ethyl acetate	✿✿✿
	■

✿ Bioeffluent removal per plant
■ Bioeffluent emitted per student

complex organic structures found in leaves and other jungle debris. Plant leaves can also absorb gaseous organic substances and digest or translocate them to their roots where they serve as food for microbes. Transpiration is another means plants have of moving air-polluting substances to microbes around their roots. High transpiration rates create convection currents that cause air flow. As water rapidly moves from roots up through plants, air is pulled down into the soil around the roots. This is one means by which plants can supply oxygen and gaseous nitrogen to their root microbes. Nitrogen gas can also be converted by root microbes into nitrate, a plant food.

PERSONAL BREATHING ZONES

A personal breathing zone is an area of 0.17 to 0.23 cu. m (6 – 8 cu. ft), surrounding an individual. These are usually areas where an individual remains for several hours, such as at a desk or computer, watching television or asleep. Plants placed within a personal breathing zone can add humidity, remove bioeffluents and chemical toxins, and suppress airborne microbes. These benefits are in addition to their aesthetic and psychological values.

Dry air, typical of the indoor environment during winter, irritates sensitive membranes in the nose and throat, increasing susceptibility to assaults by airborne chemicals, viruses, mould spores, dust and allergens.

Plants also release phytochemicals that suppress mould spores and bacteria found in the ambient air. Recent research findings show that plant-filled rooms contained 50 to 60 per cent fewer airborne moulds and bacteria than rooms without plants. This effect is illustrated in the table (right), which compares the number of microbe colonies in rooms with and without houseplants. Plants probably release phytochemicals to protect themselves from attack by airborne microbes.

After more than 15 years of extensive research in both laboratory and "real world" environments, we now have a basic understanding of how plants function to improve indoor air quality. Most houseplants, whose origins began underneath the canopy of tropical rainforests, have evolved over millions of years. These plants naturally thrive in dimly lit, warm and humid environments. Nature has equipped these plants with the ability to culture microbes on and around their roots that can degrade

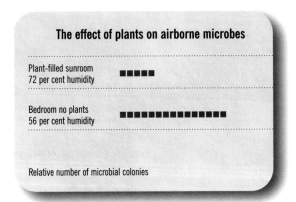

The effect of plants on airborne microbes

Plant-filled sunroom 72 per cent humidity	■■■■■
Bedroom no plants 56 per cent humidity	■■■■■■■■■■■■■■■

Relative number of microbial colonies

Pollutants in the air are absorbed through microscopic openings in leaves called stomata.

Water vapour is emitted into the atmosphere from plant leaves through a process called transpiration.

Convection currents set up by leaf transpiration transport pollutants to the root zone.

Root microbes (e.g., Pseudomonas sp.) biodegrade the pollutants into structures that can be used as a source of food for the microbes and the plant.

Enhanced, fan-assisted planters have also been developed by Wolverton Environmental Services, Inc. that have the VOC-removal capacity of approximately 200 houseplants. These filters are highly effective within personal breathing zones.

AIR PURIFICATION ON A LARGE SCALE

Although houseplants can help clean the air within a personal breathing zone, providing clean, healthy air for an entire building is also desirable. Increased ventilation is neither efficient, cost-effective nor environmentally responsible. Allowing materials to off-gas before installation is helpful, but many products continue to off-gas for years.

If one views a building as having its own ecosystem, then the use of plants to improve IAQ is certainly feasible. While maybe not the total solution, houseplants can certainly be included as an integral component in creating a healthy building. To accomplish this goal, architects and builders must design with plants in mind. Often, plants are only an afterthought to fill a void in a vacant corner, or they are added later by the occupants in an attempt to create a link with nature.

To prove the concept of a building as its own ecosystem, a 113 sq. m (1,218 sq. ft) extension to my home in Picayune, Mississippi, included an indoor air purification/wastewater treatment system. An L-shaped hydroponic planter, built around the outer interior walls of the sun-room, serves four main functions:

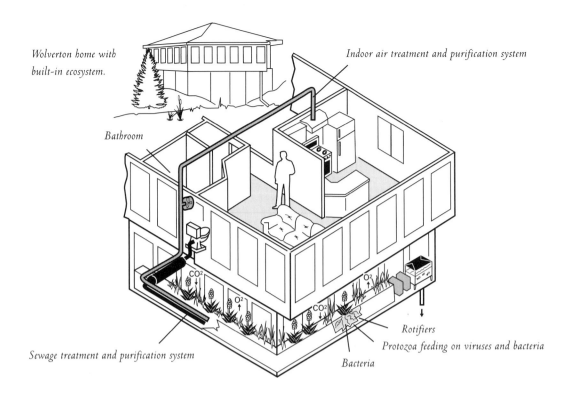

Wolverton home with built-in ecosystem.

Indoor air treatment and purification system

Bathroom

CO_2

O_2

CO_2

O_2

Rotifiers

Protozoa feeding on viruses and bacteria

Sewage treatment and purification system

Bacteria

aesthetics, air purification, humidity control, and treatment of wastewater from an adjacent bathroom. A central heat pump distributes air from the sun-room throughout the extension. This unique, patented system also has an exhaust-gas scrubber process built into the plant-root area. Odours and other gases from the kitchen and bathroom are removed by exhaust fans into a portion of the planter containing highly absorbent filtering media, such as activated carbon. Once the noxious gases have been trapped by the filter media, plant-root microbes utilize them as a source of energy and food. In essence, plants and microbes create a continuous biological cleaning process. Plants, common in interior landscape designs, fill the planter. Their sole source of nutrients and water is supplied by a bathroom and toilet. However, planter/filter units can also connect to tap water/nutrient systems instead of wastewater, if desired. This system, built in 1989, has exceeded all expectations in functionality, ease of maintenance, and

rainforest-like ambience.

The system is monitored for temperature, relative humidity, and airborne microbes. Humidity levels are sustained within a comfortable range of 40 to 60 per cent utilizing a standard heating and cooling heat pump system. VOCs are below detection limits. More importantly, no member of the household has experienced any of the symptoms associated with sick building syndrome. Airborne levels of moulds and bacteria remain 50 to 60 per cent below levels found in plant-free rooms.

The first public building to use plants for the specific purpose of creating a healthy indoor environment, is a maths/science building on the campus of Northeast Mississippi Community College in Booneville, Mississippi. State and college officials wanted a building that would be a model of energy efficiency and environmental technology. The plant-based air-purification system became an integral component of this healthy building. This small-town college took a giant step towards the 21st century by using an innovative, cost-effective means of maintaining energy efficiency and providing excellent indoor air quality.

The building itself is a teaching tool for various scientific disciplines. An atrium-based planter system, located on the second floor, uses the ability of houseplants to clean the air within a 372 sq. m (4,000 sq. ft) section of the building that houses offices and conference rooms. Sewage from two faculty restrooms serves as the source of water and nutrients for the plants. As the wastewater slowly passes underneath the plants, it is purified. Any excess wastewater is gravity-fed to the exterior landscaping for further treatment. Ventilation within this section of the building is reduced and the air recirculated. Since occupancy in 1993, there have been no indoor air quality complaints. In fact, office space in this portion of the building is in the greatest demand as everyone enjoys the superior air quality and aesthetic beauty only living plants can provide. The ultimate goal for every building is to provide a comfortable, productive environment in as cost-effective a manner as possible.

The University of Mississippi is constructing a Center for Water and Wetlands Resources that will also utilize plants for indoor air and wastewater purification. This facility promises to be the most complex and comprehensive use of plants for cleaning air and wastewater to date.

The most impressive evidence that a vast array of

Plants influence air quality within a personal breathing zone.

houseplants can create a healthy, euphoric indoor environment is the Opryland Hotel in Nashville, Tennessee. Their indoor gardens play a major role in the hotel's success. Two massive six-storey, semi-tropical gardens sprawl over 4.9 ha (12 acres), and 0.81 ha (2 acres) under glass supply natural lighting. Approximately 18,000 indoor plants, representing 600 species, grow in a jungle-like setting. This comfortable environment maintains a year-round temperature of 22°C (71°F) and a healthy 55 to 60 per cent humidity. The popularity of the original gardens has led to the construction of a new 1.6-hectare (4-acre) glass-enclosed area called the Delta. This area encompasses a river system and lake, and includes plants native to southern delta environments.

From individual houseplants in personal breathing zones to advancements in planter/filter bio-technology, plants are helping to win the battle for clean, healthy air in the indoor environment. These processes, which closely balance plants, microorganisms and humans, are as nature intended.

Research data and real-world applications that prove the effectiveness of plants in improving indoor air quality are slowly changing how most people view their favourite houseplants. Houseplants are no longer luxuries, but essential to health. They are nature's "eco-friendly" living air-purifiers, with years of documented scientific evidence to prove it.

4

"Horticulture again – now in the guise of space biology – has reestablished the essential connection between plants and people. Horticulture must increase in importance, in schools, in homes, in communities, to underscore the interconnectedness of the living world and to improve the beauty and the quality of life here on earth.

Professor Jules Janick, Purdue University

A GROWER'S GUIDE

Most houseplants thrive in broadly the same temperatures that we enjoy. Others require special arrangements, such as a change in temperature when the seasons change or a cool location for a rest period. Most plants will grow in a temperature range of 18 to 24°C (65 – 75°F). Fluctuations of a few degrees on either side are not harmful and most plants will enjoy a slight drop in temperature at night.

Avoid placing plants too close to windows. The air near a window can be much hotter or colder than the room temperature. Also keep plants away from fireplaces, radiators and heating or cooling vents. No plant likes blasts of hot or cold air.

HUMIDITY

Moisture in the atmosphere is as important to human health and well-being as it is to houseplants. The ideal humidity for plants and humans ranges between 35 and 65 per cent. Humidity levels are closely linked to air temperatures: the warmer the air, the more rapidly moisture is lost.

Mechanical humidifiers can be used to add moisture to the air. However, a strict regimen of proper cleaning must be followed to prevent the growth of disease-causing microorganisms. An alternative method of adding humidity is to set plants in pebble-filled trays and add water. However, open, stagnant water sitting in a warm room is an open invitation to grow mould and mildew. This method is not recommended when air quality is of concern.

Probably the simplest method of providing humidity for a plant is to mist its leaves regularly. In extremely dry conditions, misting more than once a day may be necessary. Care should be taken not to wet carpeting or other floor coverings. Grouping plants together is also helpful. Plant leaves will catch and hold transpired moisture from neighbouring plants. Remember that plants themselves are natural humidifiers! The drier the air, the more moisture a plant gives off through the process of transpiration.

AIR CIRCULATION

The movement of fresh, moist air helps plants to breathe. When plants are grouped together, allow room for air circulation. When air is unable to circulate, plants are more susceptible to fungal disease and pests. Avoid draughts or sudden changes in temperature around plants. The accumulation of dust on leaves can clog the stomata (the microscopic openings on the leaves), which may result in slower plant growth. Misting helps to remove dust, but perhaps the best method for most plants is to simply wipe leaves with a damp cloth. Do not use a dry duster or soft brush as this causes dust to become airborne.

LIGHT

All plants need light, but the amount of light needed varies with each genus and species. Generally, plants that bloom, bear fruit or have variegated foliage need more light than plants with plain green foliage. Most of the houseplants we know today originally came from tropical and subtropical regions. A variety of lighting conditions is found within these regions, from dimly lit areas underneath the canopy of rainforests to bright, open grasslands and even mountainous terrains. Even though a plant has been removed to a different location, it continues to need lighting conditions similar to those in its native habitat or it may not survive.

Natural light The question is not whether natural sunlight is best, but how much exposure to sunlight is needed and for how long. The amount of light within a room or even a section of a room changes throughout the day. Usually plants from arid regions, such as cacti and succulents, are the only ones that can survive in direct sunlight all day. Some can withstand direct light for short periods before burning. Others prefer indirect or filtered light, as through a net curtain. A basic understanding of a plant's light needs will help in maintaining a healthy plant.

Incandescent light Incandescent bulbs are those used in most conventional domestic light fittings. Incandescent lights emit a high proportion of red rays, which are needed by flowering plants. However, the total output of blue and violet rays is insufficient. Therefore, incandescent light is not suitable as the sole light source for growing plants, but may be used in combination with fluorescent light,

Houseplants for different lighting conditions

Common name	Botanical name	Common name	Botanical name
FULL SUN			
Aloe vera	*Aloe barbandensis*	Kalanchoe	*Kalanchoe blossfeldiana*
Croton	*Codiaeum variegatum pictum*	Norfolk Island pine	*Araucaria heterophylla*
Dwarf banana	*Musa cavendishii*	Tulip	*Tulipa gesneriana*
Ficus alii	*Ficus macleilandii "Alii"*	Wax begonia	*Begonia semperflorens*
Florist's mum	*Chrysanthemum morifolium*	Weeping fig	*Ficus benjamina*
Gerbera daisy	*Gerbera jamesonii*		
SEMI-SUN			
Aloe vera	*Aloe barbandensis*	Gerbera daisy	*Gerbera jamesonii*
Anthurium	*Anthurium andraeanum*	Kimberley queen fern	*Nephrolepis obliterata*
Areca palm	*Chrysalidocarpus lutescens*	Lady palm	*Rhapis excelsa*
Arrowhead vine	*Syngonium podophyllum*	Lily turf	*Liriope spicata*
Bamboo palm	*Chamaedorea seifritzii*	Norfolk Island pine	*Araucaria heterophylla*
Boston fern	*Nephrolepis exaltata "Bostoniensis"*	Oakleaf ivy	*Cissus rhombifolia "Ellen Danika"*
Christmas cactus	*Schlumbergera bridgesii*	Parlour palm	*Chamaedorea elegans*
Easter cactus	*Schlumbergera rhipsalidopsis*	Peace lily	*Spathiphyllum sp.*
Croton	*Codiaeum variegatum pictum*	Prayer plant	*Maranta leuconeura "Kerchoveana"*
Dendrobium orchid	*Dendrobium sp.*	Rubber plant	*Ficus robusta*
Dumb cane	*Dieffenbachia camilla*	Snake plant	*Sansevieria trifasciata*
Dumb cane	*Dieffenbachia "Exotica Compacta"*	Spider plant	*Chlorophytum comosum "Vittatum"*
Dwarf banana	*Musa cavendishii*	Tulip	*Tulipa gesneriana*
Dwarf date palm	*Phoenix roebelenii*	Urn plant	*Aechmea fasciata*
English ivy	*Hedera helix*	Wax begonia	*Begonia semperflorens*
Ficus alii	*Ficus macleilandii "Alii"*	Weeping fig	*Ficus benjamina*
Florist's mum	*Chrysanthemum morifolium*		

Houseplants for different lighting conditions

Common name	Botanical name	Common name	Botanical name
SEMI-SHADE			
Arrowhead vine	*Syngonium podophyllum*	Lacy tree philodendron	*Philodendron selloum*
Boston fern	*Nephrolepis exaltata*	Lily turf	*Liriope spicata*
Chinese evergreen	*Aglaonema crispum*	Moth orchid	*Phalenopsis* sp.
Corn plant	*Dracaena fragrans*	Norfolk Island pine	*Araucaria heterophylla*
Croton	*Codiaeum variegatum pictum*	Oakleaf ivy	*Cissus rhombifolia* "Ellen Danika"
Cyclamen	*Cyclamen persicum*	Parlour palm	*Chamaedorea elegans*
Dragon tree	*Dracaena marginata*	Peace lily	*Spathiphyllum* sp.
Dumb cane	*Dieffenbachia camilla*	Peacock plant	*Calathea makoyana*
Dumb cane	*Dieffenbachia* "Exotica Compacta"	Poinsettia	*Euphorbia pulcherrima*
Dwarf azalea	*Rhododendron simsii* "Compacta"	Prayer plant	*Maranta leuconeura* "Kerchoveana"
Elephant ear philodendron	*Philodendron domesticum*	Red emerald philodendron	*Philodendron erubescens*
English ivy	*Hedera helix*	Rubber plant	*Ficus robusta*
Golden pothos	*Epipremnum aureum*	Schefflera	*Brassaia actinophylla*
Heart-leaf philodendron	*Philodendron oxycardium*	Snake plant	*Sansevieria trifasciata*
Janet Craig	*Dracaena deremensis* "Janet Craig"	Spider plant	*Chlorophytum comosum* "Vittatum"
Kimberley queen fern	*Nephrolepis obliterata*	Warneckei	*Dracaena deremensis* "Warneckei"
King of hearts	*Homalomena wallisii*		

Common name	Botanical name	Common name	Botanical name
SHADE			
Arrowhead vine	*Syngonium podophyllum*	Heart-leaf philodendron	*Philodendron oxycardium*
Chinese evergreen	*Aglaonema crispum*	King of hearts	*Homalomena wallisii*
Elephant ear philodendron	*Philodendron domesticum*	Red emerald philodendron	*Philodendron erubescens*
Golden pothos	*Epipremnum aureum*	Snake plant	*Sansevieria trifasciata*

without the presence of sunlight, for growing flowering plants.

Fluorescent light Fluorescent lamps are commonly used in offices and, to a lesser extent, homes. The light differs from that produced by incandescent bulbs in that it contains a high proportion of foliage-producing blue rays. Plants grown primarily for their foliage can be maintained using fluorescent light alone. Modified fluorescent lamps are available that emit blue, violet and red. Cool-white fluorescent bulbs are more commonly used primarily because they are less expensive and they do not burn or dry out tender foliage as do incandescent lights.

Metal halide light Metal halide lamps produce light several times more intense than that produced by incandescent lamps. The most popular halide lamps emit a full and complete spectrum of light. Balanced blue and white light provides plants with everything they need for healthy growth and flowering. Halide lamps are commonly used for growing large plants indoors.

LIGHTING CATEGORIES FOR HOUSEPLANTS

Although houseplants can be grown successfully using only artificial light, most indoor plants are grown near windows using natural light, supplemented with artificial light. The following four lighting categories are used throughout this book. The tables on pp. 32–3 list the preferred lighting conditions of the 50 plants described in the second part of this book.

Full sun Describes an area that receives at least five hours a day of direct sunlight. This is the brightest lighting category. Very few houseplants can withstand full sun for the entire day. Sun rays may be magnified by window panes and the temperature can reach levels that burn foliage. Even plants that enjoy direct sunlight should be placed away from the window pane and should be given some protection in summer.

Semi-sun Describes an area that receives only a couple of hours of direct sunlight in winter. For the greatest proportion of the day this area receives bright reflected or indirect light. Most flowering plants will bloom in these conditions.

Semi-shade Describes an area that receives a great deal of bright, indirect light without any direct sun. This light is usually filtered by net curtains, trees, shrubs or overhangs. If provided with additional artificial lighting, some flowering plants will bloom. Most foliage plants prefer this category of light.

Shade Describes an area that receives no direct sunlight and that is somewhat dark even at midday. However, there should be sufficient indirect light to cast a shadow. Only a few foliage houseplants can survive for long in these lighting conditions. They need either supplemental lighting or periodic rotation to a brighter location.

GROWTH MEDIA

Hydroculture Growing plants in a water solution has been practised for more than 50 years. This technique whereby water and nutrients flow through plant roots is termed hydroponics. During World War II, hydroponic techniques were used to grow fresh vegetables for US troops stationed in the Pacific Islands. In Europe and the United States, large greenhouse operations use hydroponics to grow flowers and vegetables for urban markets.

The hydroponic technique of growing houseplants in a water-tight container filled with support substrate other than soil is commonly referred to as hydroculture. Water and nutrients are supplied below the surface of the substrate. Often the terms hydroponics and hydroculture are used interchangeably.

In Europe most houseplants are grown commercially using hydroculture techniques. However, few US commercial growers use these methods. They are perceived by many as complicated or too scientific. It is also mistakenly believed that only the use of clay aggregates from Europe proves successful. However, inexpensive expanded clay aggregates and any of the highly porous, igneous rocks (lava, pumice, etc.) provide inexpensive substrates for hydroculture.

The purpose of the substrate is not only to act as a support media for the plant, but also to assist the movement of water and nutrients to plant roots. Highly porous substrates act as wicks for drawing moisture from the water reservoir up to plant roots. This method allows plants that love constant moisture to extend their roots deep into the moist zone, while non-moisture-loving plants can extend their roots into the drier zones.

As more people purchase houseplants for the primary purpose of improving indoor air quality, the use of hydroculture will surely increase. There are significant benefits associated with hydroculture. Hydroculture is much less messy since there is no soil involved. It takes the guesswork out of watering. Simply maintain the water between minimum and maximum on the water level indicator. Oxygen and other atmospheric gases are more easily drawn down to the root area, therefore, houseplants grown in hydroculture are more effective air purifiers. Because plants are watered from the bottom and the surface remains dry, fungal or mould problems are virtually nonexistent. Pest infestations can also be greatly reduced.

Less frequent applications of fertilizer are needed in hydroculture. Minerals naturally found in tap water concentrate as a result of water loss through evaporation and transpiration. Always introduce water and nutrients through a water-fill tube. Watering from the top encourages salt crystals to form on the top layer of substrate. If salt crystals form, remove a 5 to 7.5 cm (2 – 3-in) layer and soak in hot water to remove the salt build-up.

Some plants are salt-sensitive and others are more adept at dealing with salts. For instance, an areca palm can channel salt and other minerals into selected branches. Once saturated, these branches die and must be removed. The lady palm absorbs and translocates excess salts to its leaf tips. Trimming dead leaf tips with pinking shears will retain the natural, saw-toothed appearance of the leaves. Other plants use similar means to remove excess minerals from hydroculture media. The accumulation of minerals depends primarily upon the plant's transpiration rate and the concentration of minerals in tap water. Many plants can grow for years in hydroculture before salt build-up occurs.

Sub-irrigation Sub-irrigation is the technique of growing plants in soil-filled, watertight containers in which water is introduced below the soil surface. This system is similar to hydroculture except that soil is used instead of substrate. Sub-irrigation is rapidly gaining favour, especially in the commercial interior plantscape industry. However, it is less frequently used by individuals for growing houseplants in the home.

An advantage of sub-irrigation systems is that water is drawn from the reservoir at a measured rate. This system avoids the dry/wet/dry cycles common with manual top watering. Moreover, minerals are retained in the soil and not flushed into the drain pan as with standard containers. Apart from the messiness of handling soil, among the disadvantages of sub-irrigation methods is the fact than exposed soil surfaces can support growth of moulds. Soil has greater density than

hydroponic media and resists air penetration. It is therefore more difficult for oxygen and other atmospheric gases to reach plant roots. As a result, plants grow more slowly and they are less effective in the removal of toxins from the air.

Standard containers Standard containers are the traditional way of growing houseplants. The planter consists of a pot with drainage holes in the bottom and a corresponding drain pan or saucer to catch excess water. Water is poured onto the soil surface. Top-watering leaches minerals from the soil into the drain pan. Therefore, more frequent applications of fertilizer are necessary. Standard containers have the advantage that containers and potting mixes and plants are readily available. In addition, for

Water Fill Pipe

Potting Soil

Water Level

Water reservoir

Sub-irrigation plant container

Water level indicator

Expanded Clay Aggregates

Water Level

Water reservoir

Hydroculture plant container

salt-sensitive houseplants, the leaching out of minerals is advantageous. A disadvantage of standard containers is that watering is largely guesswork. Overwatering results in root rot and mould growth in drain pans and on floor coverings. Underwatering causes stress to the plant. Over-damp top soil also encourages mould growth and air circulation to the roots is reduced. Minerals leach out of the soil requiring more frequent feeding.

PESTS

The insects most commonly found on houseplants are mealybugs, spider mites, aphids and scale insects.

Spider mites These tiny insects are so small they are hardly visible to the naked eye. Dry, warm conditions promote their growth. They produce fine webs on the undersides of leaves and suck out plant juices. Infested plants become stunted and may die. To confirm their presence, use a magnifying glass or shake a plant branch over a white sheet of paper. If dark specks resembling dust fall on the paper and then can be seen to move, your plant is infested with spider mites.

Mealybugs These are soft, powder-covered insects that look like specks of cotton. Sucking insects, they cause stunted or distorted growth in plants. Mealybugs produce a sticky substance that can encourage the growth of sooty mould.

Scale insects Scale insects are soft or hard, reddish grey or brown, with round or oval bodies. They are slow-moving and resemble tiny turtles. They secrete a sticky substance that promotes the growth of sooty mould.

Aphids Aphids, or plant lice, are tiny, soft-bodied insects that cluster on buds, stems or new plant growth. Aphids, like mealybugs and scale insects, also secrete a sticky substance, called honeydew. The presence of aphids results in curled, distorted leaves or flowers.

PEST MANAGEMENT

Careful inspection of plants before bringing them indoors is certainly advisable. Meeting a plant's environmental needs reduces plant stress and a healthy plant is less vulnerable to attack. When pest control is necessary, non-toxic or less toxic insecticides can offer effective control. These include plant-derived insecticidal soaps, surgical spirit or homemade solutions.

Natural pyrethrum insecticidal spray is extracted from the dried flower head of the chrysanthemum and is relatively safe. However, the recently introduced synthetic pyrethrum is less desirable.

A 0.2 per cent solution of mild washing-up liquid is generally an effective method of washing plant leaves. Cotton buds dipped in surgical spirit are good way of removing spider mites, mealybugs, scale insects and aphids.

You can try making your own non-toxic spray solution. The following ingredients, mixed into a spray bottle, and shaken vigorously, can be sprayed onto plant leaves:
2 teaspoons (10 ml) vegetable oil
$1/_8$ teaspoon (0.6 ml) washing-up liquid
230 ml (8 fl. oz) warm tap water

When choosing plants for your home, make sure you are aware of their care needs and any particular problems to which they may be susceptible. To help you make your choice, the next chapter describes the characteristics of 50 houseplants individually.

5

THE PLANTS

On the following pages information is

provided on 50 houseplants that have been

tested for their ecological benefits. These

plants have been graded according to ease of growth and

maintenance, resistance to pests, efficiency at removing chemical

vapours, and transpiration rates. Each plant has been given an

overall rating, based on its score in each category. Those plants

with the highest overall rating are listed first. Where two or more

plants have an equal overall rating, priority is given to those that

have the best performance in the removal of chemicals from the air.

ARECA PALM

(*Chrysalidocarpus lutescens*)

Also known as yellow palm or butterfly palm, the areca palm is one of the most popular and graceful palms. It is tolerant of the indoor environment, releases copious amounts of moisture into the air, removes chemical toxins, and is also beautiful to look at. What more could one ask of a houseplant!

One of the faster-growing palms, the areca features a cluster of cane-like stalks that produce feathery, yellow-green fronds. Because of its all-around good qualities, the areca is commonly found in commercial settings as well as in the home. An underplanting of golden pothos or English ivy adds to its aesthetic appeal.

In a home setting, a 1.8-m (6-ft) areca palm transpires approximately one litre (2 pints) of water every 24 hours. The areca is consistently rated among the best houseplants for removing all indoor air toxins tested. It also has the unique ability to move salt accumulations to selected branches. When saturated, these branches die and should be quickly removed. Its high marks in all rated categories make the areca one of the top "eco-friendly" houseplants.

FAMILY

Arecaceae (palm).

ORIGIN

Madagascar.

LIGHT

Semi-sun.

TEMPERATURE

18–24°C (65–75°F).

PESTS AND PROBLEMS

Spider mites and brown tips on fronds from over-dry atmosphere.

CARE

Keep the root ball damp. Provide a complete fertilizer on a regular basis, except in winter. Mist regularly to give it a fresh appearance and to provide humidity to discourage insect infestation.

MEDIA

A good loam-based potting mix is needed for standard containers. However, because the areca palm has a very high transpiration rate, hydroculture or sub-irrigation methods are also highly recommended. These methods require less frequent watering.

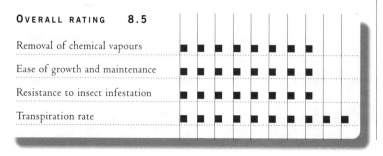

OVERALL RATING	8.5
Removal of chemical vapours	
Ease of growth and maintenance	
Resistance to insect infestation	
Transpiration rate	

LADY PALM

(Rhapis excelsa)

This large palm has fans 15 to 30 cm (6 – 12 in) wide that consist of between four and ten thick, shiny leaves. The leaves are connected to a brown, hairy main trunk by thin, arching stems. Lady palm is one of the easiest houseplants to care for and is highly resistant to attack by most plant insects. It is also one of the best plants for improving indoor air quality. It grows slowly and is easy to maintain. The lady palm is so popular in the United States that some commercial nurseries deal exclusively in its production.

When grown using sub-irrigation or hydroculture and tap water, some concentration of salt and minerals may accumulate in its leaf tips causing them to turn brown. The leaf tips can be trimmed with pinking shears to remove the salt build-up and leave the tips with their natural green, saw-toothed appearance.

FAMILY

Arecaeae (palm).

ORIGIN

Southern China.

LIGHT

Semi-sun.

TEMPERATURE

16–21°C (60–70°F); do not allow to drop below 10°C (50°F) in winter.

PESTS AND PROBLEMS

Usually pest free. Occasionally spider mites. Too dry a location causes fronds to dry and turn brown.

CARE

Water generously in spring and summer. In a warm, dry winter indoor environment, it may be necessary to water more frequently. Feed monthly with diluted liquid fertilizer.

MEDIA

Soil, hydroculture or sub-irrigation.

OVERALL RATING   8.5

Removal of chemical vapours	
Ease of growth and maintenance	
Resistance to insect infestation	
Transpiration rate	

BAMBOO PALM

(*Chamaedorea seifrizii*)

Most members of the palm family are easy to care for and continue to be popular houseplants. The bamboo palm is no exception and is a long-standing favourite in homes and commercial establishments. It produces clusters of small, slender canes. Its graceful fans and rich green colour give it an overall lacy appearance. A bamboo palm can reach a height of about 1.8 m (6 ft).

Bamboo palms are often chosen over areca palms by commercial interiorscapers because they are more resistant to insect infestation. They add a peaceful, tropical feeling wherever they are placed.

In terms of its atmospheric benefits, the bamboo palm has an excellent overall rating and one of the highest transpiration ratings. It pumps much needed moisture into the indoor atmosphere, especially during winter months when heating systems dry the air. This palm is also one of the top-rated plants tested for the removal of benzene, trichloroethylene and formaldehyde.

FAMILY

Arecaceae (palm).

ORIGIN

Mexico.

LIGHT

Semi-sun.

TEMPERATURE

16–24°C (60–75°F); not below 10°C (50°F) in winter.

PESTS AND PROBLEMS

Spider mites and scale insects are a risk when the atmosphere is too dry.

CARE

Provide plenty of water during periods of active growth. In winter, when grown in standard containers, water just enough to keep the root ball moist. Wash the leaves periodically to prevent spider mites. Do not pinch out the tip of the stalks or cut off the newest frond as this will eliminate new growth.

MEDIA

In standard containers, pot in all-purpose potting mix with a little sand added to improve drainage. Because the bamboo palm has a high transpiration rate, it is easy to maintain using hydroculture or sub-irrigation methods, which require less frequent watering.

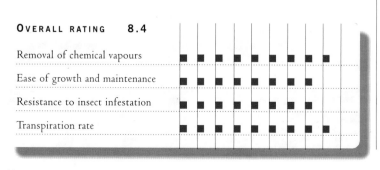

OVERALL RATING	8.4
Removal of chemical vapours	
Ease of growth and maintenance	
Resistance to insect infestation	
Transpiration rate	

RUBBER PLANT

(*Ficus robusta*)

Formerly known as *Ficus elastica*, the rubber plant was a favourite plant of the Victorians and remains equally popular today. Bred for toughness, it will survive in less light than most plants its size. It will tolerate dim light and cool temperatures. This plant is easy to grow and is especially effective at removing formaldehyde. It receives high marks in all categories and is an excellent overall houseplant.

Its common name is derived from its thick, leather-like, dark-green leaves that contain a rubber-like latex. Given proper conditions, it will eventually reach a height of 2.5 m (8 ft). Of the ficus plants tested to date, the rubber plant is the best for removing chemical toxins from the indoor environment. Favoured by architects and designers for its aesthetic value and its ease of growth, its popularity for years to come should be reinforced by its ability to remove toxins.

FAMILY

Moraceae (fig).

ORIGIN

India and Malaya.

LIGHT

Semi-sun to semi-shade.

TEMPERATURE

16–27°C (60–80°F); will tolerate temperatures as low as 5°C (40°F) for short periods.

PESTS AND PROBLEMS

In dry, centrally heated air, susceptible to attacks by scale insects, spider mites and thrips.

CARE

Feed regularly during the summer months only. Water regularly from mid summer to autumn allowing the soil to dry slightly between waterings; then water sparingly. The rubber tree does not tolerate overwatering.

MEDIA

Grows well in soil or hydroculture.

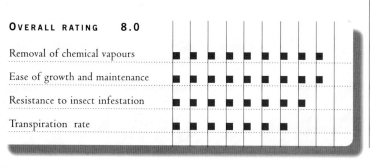

OVERALL RATING	8.0
Removal of chemical vapours	
Ease of growth and maintenance	
Resistance to insect infestation	
Transpiration rate	

DRACAENA "JANET CRAIG"

(Dracaena deremensis "Janet Craig")

The dark-green leaves of dracaena 'Janet Craig' make it a most attractive plant. It is one of the best plants for removing trichloroethylene.

Dracaena "Janet Craig" features a rosette of broad, dark-green leaves. The mature plant can reach a height of 3 m (10 ft), but can be contained by pruning. The "Compacta" is a smaller variety that reaches only 0.3 to 0.9 m (1-3 ft). While the regular variety grows quickly, the "Compacta" is a slow grower. It is also less demanding in its care requirements than the larger version. These plants can tolerate neglect and dimly lit environments.

Dracaenas are popular in office buildings and homes with contemporary interiors. "Janet Craig" is best among the dracaenas for removing chemical toxins from the indoor environment. Scoring well in all categories, it should live for decades if properly maintained.

FAMILY

Agavaceae (agave).

ORIGIN

Canary Islands, Africa, Asia and Madagascar.

LIGHT

Semi-shade; will tolerate dimly lit areas, but growth will be slow.

TEMPERATURE

Ideally, 16–24°C (60–75°F). Can survive in temperatures as low as 10°C (50°F), but leaves may yellow.

PESTS AND PROBLEMS

Usually pest resistant, but may suffer attacks of spider mites, scale insects or mealybugs in air that is too dry.

CARE

Keep soil evenly moist, but not soggy. Do not allow the root ball to dry. Provide liquid fertilizer every two weeks in spring and summer. In autumn and winter, water less often and do not feed. Mist often or wipe with a damp cloth. Do not use commercial leaf-shine products.

MEDIA

Use a commercial all-purpose potting mix, and repot every two years. Grows equally well in hydroculture.

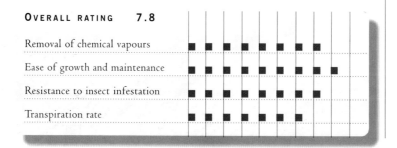

OVERALL RATING   7.8

Removal of chemical vapours

Ease of growth and maintenance

Resistance to insect infestation

Transpiration rate

ENGLISH IVY

(Hedera helix)

English ivy is often used as ground cover in public atriums or lobbies. But to add interest, try growing it in topiary form. It is ideal for use in hanging baskets. Countless varieties of ivy have been developed that offer a wide range of leaf shapes and colours. They are easy to grow and adapt to a variety of home environments. However, they do not generally do well in high temperatures.

The typical ivy leaf consists of three to five lobes, but shows differences in colouring for each variety. The variegated ivies require plenty of light otherwise they lose their colouring.

English ivy is a vigorous climber, which sends out aerial roots that attach themselves to any surface.

This plant may benefit from being outdoors for a period in spring or summer. It has an excellent overall rating and is particularly effective at removing formaldehyde.

FAMILY
Araliaceae (aralia).

ORIGIN
Asia, Europe and North Africa.

LIGHT
Semi-sun to semi-shade.

TEMPERATURE
Day: 16–21°C (60–70°F); night: 10–16°C (50–60°F).

PESTS AND PROBLEMS
Spider mites and scale insects in too warm and dry a location.

CARE
Water well in spring and summer with room-temperature water. Allow to dry slightly between waterings in autumn and winter. Feed regularly with a weak concentration fertilizer when plants are growing. Mist often, especially during winter when the air is dry.

MEDIA
Grows equally well in hydroculture or all-purpose potting mix.

OVERALL RATING	7.8

Removal of chemical vapours

Ease of growth and maintenance

Resistance to insect infestation

Transpiration rate

DWARF DATE PALM

(Phoenix roebelenii)

This palm usually reaches a maximum height of 1.5 to 2 m (5 – 6 ¹/₂ ft). However, it is a very slow grower. It produces a stately main trunk with graceful, green fans that droop elegantly. The fronds reach about 0.9 m (3 ft) and grow almost horizontally. It is best seen when given adequate space and is impressive standing alone, especially when given spot lighting. Because its natural habitat is underneath the canopy of dense, tropical forests, it adapts quite well to the low light levels and controlled temperatures of homes and offices. When its environmental needs are met, the date palm can survive for decades.

The dwarf date palm, like most other palms, has a high overall rating. It is one of the best palms for removing indoor air pollutants and is especially effective for the removal of xylene.

FAMILY

(Palm).

ORIGIN

Tropical and sub-tropical Africa and Asia.

LIGHT

Semi-sun.

TEMPERATURE

16–24°C (60–75°F); not below 10°C (50°F) in winter.

PESTS AND PROBLEMS

Spider mites in dry air. Brown fronds from overwatering or the use of hard water.

CARE

The root ball should be kept evenly moist. However, the soil can be allowed to dry between waterings in winter. This plant loves frequent misting. The date palm prefers a weekly feeding schedule, except in winter when feeding can be on a two-weekly basis.

MEDIA

The date palm is quite happy in standard indoor potting mix. Hydroculture or sub-irrigation methods are preferred because these methods require less frequent watering.

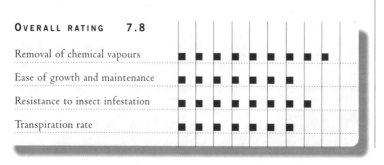

OVERALL RATING   7.8

Removal of chemical vapours

Ease of growth and maintenance

Resistance to insect infestation

Transpiration rate

FICUS ALII

(*Ficus macleilandii* "Alii")

This is a new ficus that is rapidly gaining in popularity. Its slender dark green leaves make it an extremely attractive plant. The *Ficus alii* was imported to Hawaii from Thailand by Masuo Moriwaki, a Japanese plant collector. In the early 1980s, it was brought to South Florida and first sold commercially in the mid 1980s. It is much less finicky than the *Ficus benjamina*, and is appealing both to the interior plantscape industry and to the home market.

There are three types: the standard tree, the bush (several stems from one pot), and the braids (two or three entwined trunks). Like all species of ficus, expect some leaf drop until the plant adjusts to its new location.

A magnificent large plant, its ability to help purify the air, ease of growth and resistance to insects make it an excellent choice for the home or office.

FAMILY

Moraceae (fig).

ORIGIN

Thailand.

LIGHT

Full sun and semi-sun.

TEMPERATURE

Day: 16–24°C (60–75°F); night: 13–20°C (55–68°F). Avoid draughts.

PESTS AND PROBLEMS

Rarely, scale insects or mealybugs.

CARE

When using standard containers, water thoroughly, then allow to dry between waterings. Yellowing of leaves may indicate overwatering. In a sun-room or south-facing window, fertilize monthly. In darker settings, feed less often.

MEDIA

When growing in soil, it is critical not to overwater this ficus. It is easier to maintain using sub-irrigation or hydroculture techniques.

OVERALL RATING   7.7

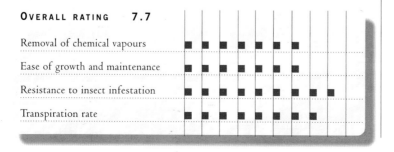

Removal of chemical vapours	
Ease of growth and maintenance	
Resistance to insect infestation	
Transpiration rate	

BOSTON FERN

(*Nephrolepis exaltata "Bostoniensis"*)

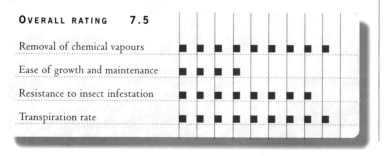

Ferns are probably one of the oldest groups of plants. Many have been found as fossils dating back to prehistoric times. They were first treasured indoors for their lush foliage in the Victorian age, and are equally popular today. The Boston fern's stiff fronds arch out, drooping downwards as they age. It is grown strictly for its foliage for it does not produce flowers. It is best displayed in a hanging basket or sitting upon a pedestal.

As an indoor plant, the Boston fern requires a certain amount of attention. It must have frequent misting and watering or the leaves will quickly turn brown and begin to drop. Of the plants tested, it is the best for removing air pollutants, especially formaldehyde, and for adding humidity to the indoor environment.

FAMILY
Polypodiaceae (fern).

ORIGIN
Tropical regions worldwide.

LIGHT
Semi-sun.

TEMPERATURE
Day: 18–24°C (65–75°F); night: 10–18°C (50–65°F).

PESTS AND PROBLEMS
Rarely scale insects, spider mites and aphids.

CARE
Feed weekly with a weak liquid fertilizer as long as the plant is producing new foliage. Feed sparingly in winter. Provide tepid water (preferably rainwater) to keep the soil moist but not soggy. Never let the root ball dry completely. Ferns love to be misted, and this is essential in hot, dry air.

MEDIA
The Boston fern probably grows best in a soil-less mix, but this method requires constant watering. It also performs well in a humus-rich potting mix and prefers to be somewhat potbound. For a less frequent watering schedule, hydroculture is the preferred choice.

OVERALL RATING   7.5

Removal of chemical vapours

Ease of growth and maintenance

Resistance to insect infestation

Transpiration rate

PEACE LILY

(*Spathiphyllum* sp.)

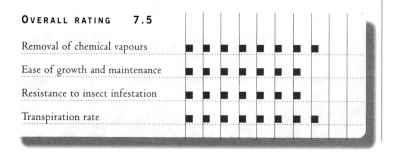

An outstanding foliage plant that also produces beautiful white spathes, the peace lily should always be included when seeking a variety of indoor plants. This plant has a high transpiration rate and enjoys the large water reservoir that hydroculture offers. It possesses all the qualities to make it one of the best indoor plants.

It sends up stiff, erect stalks that produce white spathes. These spathes unfold to reveal the plant's true flower. The flower may be cut out to prevent the release of pollen and the spathe will continue unharmed for weeks. Popular varieties include "Clevelandii", which reaches a height of 0.6 m (2 ft) and "Mauna Loa", which reaches about 0.9 m (3 feet). This plant, with its lush tropical foliage, is one of only a few plants that will reliably bloom indoors.

The peace lily excels in the removal of alcohols, acetone, trichloroethylene, benzene and formaldehyde. Its ability to remove indoor air pollutants and its excellent performance in all categories make it a most valuable houseplant.

FAMILY

Araceae (arum).

ORIGIN

Colombia and Venezuela.

LIGHT

Semi-sun to semi-shade.

TEMPERATURE

Day: 16–24°C (60–75°F); night: 13–20°C (55–68°F).

PESTS AND PROBLEMS

When air is too dry, the peace lily is vulnerable to attacks by scale insects and spider mites; occasionally mealybugs and whiteflies.

CARE

Feed regularly from spring to autumn, but less in winter. Keep the soil evenly moist during the growing season and slightly drier during the winter. Wash the leaves occasionally to prevent insect attack.

MEDIA

The peace lily grows in any growth medium, but performs exceptionally well in hydroculture.

OVERALL RATING	7.5
Removal of chemical vapours	
Ease of growth and maintenance	
Resistance to insect infestation	
Transpiration rate	

CORN PLANT

(*Dracaena fragrans* "Massangeana")

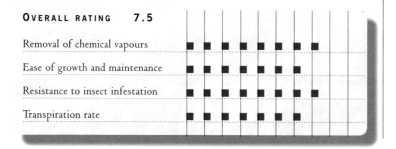

This is an excellent houseplant that rates above average in all categories. Although it prefers bright light, it can survive in dimly lit areas and works well within a contemporary decor. It is one of the most popular of all houseplants.

D. fragrans received its common name because its shiny, medium-green leaves are similar in appearance to those of the corn plant. As it matures, *D. fragrans* develops a solid woody stem. Its leaves concentrate at the top of each stem. It will on occasion send up a small spray of fragrant white flowers.

"Massangeana" is the variegated cultivar and the one most commonly found in shops. It can be identified by a broad yellow band down the centre of the leaf and is sometimes referred to as mass cane.

Indoors, a corn plant can reach a height of 3 m (10 ft). To stimulate new growth or to rejuvenate an old plant, cut back to about 20 cm (8 in). The corn plant is exceptionally effective in the removal of indoor air toxins such as formaldehyde.

FAMILY

Agavaceae (agave).

ORIGIN

Ethiopia, Guinea and Nigeria.

LIGHT

Semi-shade.

TEMPERATURE

16–24°C (60–75°F); but can survive temperatures near 10°C (50°F) for short periods.

PESTS AND PROBLEMS

Rarely attacked by pests, but susceptible to mealybugs and spider mites in dry, centrally heated air.

CARE

Keep soil moist, but not soggy. Feed regularly in spring and summer with liquid fertilizer. Water less often in winter and do not feed. Mist often or wipe leaves with a damp cloth. If brown tips occur, check care and environmental conditions and trim with scissors, taking care to keep tips in their natural shape.

MEDIA

Grows well in standard commercial potting mix. However, hydroculture requires less frequent watering and repotting.

OVERALL RATING   7.5

Removal of chemical vapours

Ease of growth and maintenance

Resistance to insect infestation

Transpiration rate

GOLDEN POTHOS

(*Epipremnum aureum*)

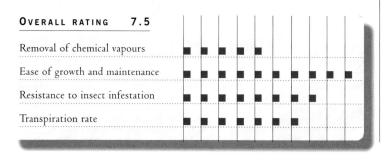

This is a vine that produces green heart-shaped leaves splashed with gold or cream colours. The plant is sometimes mistakenly sold as *Philodendron scindapus*. It is not a philodendron, although the two plants are related. Golden pothos is arguably the easiest to grow of all houseplants. It can withstand neglect and is very resistant to insect infestations. It is commonly grown in hanging baskets, but can be trained to climb. Cuttings are easily rooted in water and can then be transplanted to any potting medium.

Golden pothos grows quickly and tolerates a wide variety of environmental conditions found in the home or office. Unlike many houseplants, it does not lose its colour variations when kept in a dark setting. It is widely used in commercial applications as an underplanting for much larger plants and is often seen cascading over balconies or atrium walls. Ease of growth and maintenance and its resistance to attack by insects make golden pothos one of the best houseplants for newcomers to indoor gardening.

FAMILY

Araceae (arum).

ORIGIN

Solomon Islands.

LIGHT

Semi-shade to shade.

TEMPERATURE

18–24°C (65–75°F); do not allow to drop below 10°C (50°F) in winter.

PESTS AND PROBLEMS

Rarely, aphids and mealybugs.

CARE

Let soil dry slightly between waterings. Feed weekly during growing season (March to August). To encourage a more bushy appearance, pinch out the growth tips. Clean the leaves with a damp cloth.

MEDIA

Golden pothos performs equally well in any growing medium. However, when grown in hydroculture, repotting is rarely needed.

WARNING

The "sap" is irritant to skin and mucous membranes.

OVERALL RATING   7.5

Removal of chemical vapours

Ease of growth and maintenance

Resistance to insect infestation

Transpiration rate

KIMBERLEY QUEEN

(*Nephrolepis obliterata*)

The Kimberley queen is not as well known as the Boston fern. When it becomes more widely distributed, it may surpass its rival. Because it is not as sensitive to a lack of humidity, it is better suited for the typical indoor environment. The Kimberley queen is as effective as the Boston fern for removing toxins from the air.

Ferns evoke feelings of peaceful tranquillity. Their lush green foliage can stimulate thoughts of spring, even in the dead of winter. The Kimberley queen has graceful, drooping fronds. It is more tolerant of dry air than some other ferns, and thus does not drop as many leaves. Nevertheless, a regular schedule of misting and watering is necessary.

Kimberley queen is highly effective for the removal of harmful atmospheric pollutants, especially formaldehyde and alcohols. Its high transpiration rates make it one of the best natural humidifiers of all houseplants tested. These characteristics give the Kimberley queen fern an excellent overall rating.

FAMILY

Polypodiaceae (fern).

ORIGIN

Tropics.

LIGHT

Semi-sun to semi-shade.

TEMPERATURE

Day: 18–24°C (65–75°F); night: 10–18°C (50–65°F).

PESTS AND PROBLEMS

Rarely, scale insects, spider mites and aphids.

CARE

Apply diluted liquid fertilizer as long as it is producing new fronds. Keep the soil moist, but not wet. Never allow the root ball to dry completely. Frequent misting is necessary in dry, centrally heated air. Remove old or discoloured fronds.

MEDIA

In standard containers, a humus-rich potting mix or a soil-less mix is best. It prefers to be somewhat potbound. If grown using hydroculture or sub-irrigation, less frequent watering is required.

OVERALL RATING   7.4

Removal of chemical vapours

Ease of growth and maintenance

Resistance to insect infestation

Transpiration rate

64

FLORIST'S MUM

(Chrysanthemum morifolium)

Florist's mum provides a brilliant display of colours. They are often used to provide splashes of colour in shopping malls, office buildings and other commercial settings. It is generally considered a houseplant only while in bloom. Commercial growers apply dwarfing chemicals and manipulate the day/night cycle to induce flowering at a given time. As a result, small plants with large flowers are available all year round.

With a cool location, adequate lighting and frequent watering, this plant should bloom for six to eight weeks. Once blooming has peaked, the plants are rotated out.

Florist's mum is one of the best flowering or seasonal plants for removing formaldehyde, benzene and ammonia from the atmosphere.

FAMILY

Compositae (composite).

ORIGIN

China and Japan.

LIGHT

Full sun and semi-sun (bright light is essential, but avoid midday sun as the heat may age the blooms prematurely).

TEMPERATURE

Day: 16–18°C (60–65°F); night: 7–10°C (45–50°F).

PESTS AND PROBLEMS

Aphids and spider mites are a risk when the air is too warm and dry.

CARE

During the growing season, provide adequate water to keep the root ball slightly damp. Feed with a complete fertilizer weekly.

MEDIA

Use standard commercial potting mix.

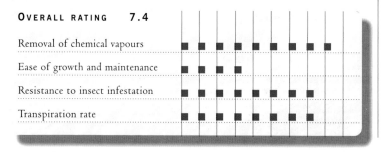

OVERALL RATING   7.4

Removal of chemical vapours

Ease of growth and maintenance

Resistance to insect infestation

Transpiration rate

GERBERA DAISY

(*Gerbera jamesonii*)

The gerbera daisy has handsome sparkling flowers, which in its natural state are yellow, red or orange. However, commercial growers have also produced pink, white, salmon, cream and crimson flowers. It has somewhat leathery leaves and sends up sturdy stems that hold its flowers. This South African perennial was named after Traugott Gerber, an 18th century German physician and naturalist. It provides summer-long colour in gardens and a wealth of long-lasting cut flowers. If brought indoors in the autumn and kept on a cool window ledge, it will continue to bloom all winter.

This plant was included in the early NASA studies and proved to be extremely effective in removing chemical vapours from the air. Its colourful array of flowers, combined with its high transpiration rate and ability to remove toxic gases, makes it a highly valued seasonal indoor plant.

FAMILY

Compositae (composite).

ORIGIN

Southern Africa.

LIGHT

Full sun to semi-sun (bright light is essential, but protect from midday sun as this may age the blooms prematurely).

TEMPERATURE

Day: 16–18°C (60–65°F); night: 7–10°C (45–50°F).

PESTS AND PROBLEMS

Aphids and spider mite infestation may occur when the air is too warm and dry. Susceptible to root rot from overwatering.

CARE

Keep the soil evenly moist, not soggy. Feed regularly during its growing season with a complete fertilizer.

MEDIA

Use standard commercial potting mix.

OVERALL RATING   7.3

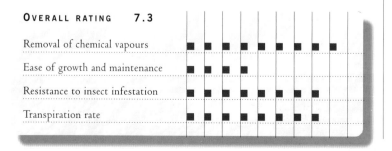

Removal of chemical vapours

Ease of growth and maintenance

Resistance to insect infestation

Transpiration rate

DRACAENA "WARNECKEI"

(Dracaena deremensis "Warneckei")

Dracaena "Warneckei" is popular with the interior plantscape industry, owing to its tolerance of the low light levels and dry air commonly found in commercial buildings. However, it is also a favourite plant for the home. Especially effective in the removal of benzene, it is an excellent overall houseplant.

"Warneckei" features leaves 0.6 m (2 ft) long and about 5 cm (2 in) wide. These are green with white and grey-green stripes. It is slower growing than the "Janet Craig", but can grow to a height of about 3 m (10 ft) indoors. It can be contained by pruning at any time. The "Compacta" is a smaller variety that only reaches 0.3 to 0.9 m (1 – 3 ft), but has similar markings.

If the tips of the leaves become brown, check care and environmental conditions. Trim the dead tips with scissors, taking care to retain their natural shape.

FAMILY

Agavaceae (agave).

ORIGIN

Tropical regions of Africa.

LIGHT

Semi-shade.

TEMPERATURE

16–24°C (60–75°F); will tolerate temperatures as low as 10°C (50°F) for short periods.

PESTS AND PROBLEMS

Root rot if too cold or damp. Occasionally attacks of spider mites, scale insects and mealybugs if the air becomes too dry.

CARE

Keep evenly moist. Avoid extremes or leaves may drop. Feed every two weeks in spring and summer. Water less often in winter and do not feed. Mist often or wipe leaves with a damp cloth or sponge. Do not use leaf-shine products.

MEDIA

Grows well in an all-purpose commercial potting mix that drains well. Thrives in hydroculture, which requires a less frequent watering schedule.

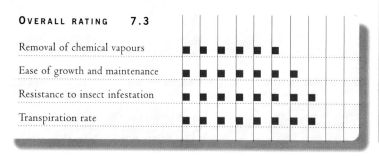

OVERALL RATING	7.3	
Removal of chemical vapours		
Ease of growth and maintenance		
Resistance to insect infestation		
Transpiration rate		

DRAGON TREE

(Dracaena marginata)

The dragon tree is one of the best known and easiest to grow of the dracaenas. It has been used as a houseplant since the early 1960s, and owing to its durability, is also found in lobbies, entrance-ways and atriums of public buildings. It has smooth grey, erect canes. Its narrowing leaves are about 0.6 m (2 ft) long and 1.3 cm (¹/₂ in) wide, and cluster at the end of each cane. These thin leaves are a deep, glossy green with red edges along the margins. The cultivar "Tricolor", introduced in the early 1970s, is striped with green, pink and cream. *D. marginata* tolerates lowlight levels and dry winter air, making it ideal for most home environments.

The dragon tree is an effective air-cleaner and is among the best plants for removing xylene and trichloroethylene.

FAMILY

Agavaceae (agave).

ORIGIN

Madagascar.

LIGHT

Semi-shade.

TEMPERATURE

16–24°C (60–75°F); tolerates a nighttime temperature as low as 10°C (50°F) for short periods.

PESTS AND PROBLEMS

Rarely attacked by pests. In dry, centrally heated air, may suffer attacks of spider mites.

CARE

Keep soil moist but not soggy. Feed regularly in spring and summer with liquid fertilizer or slow-release pellets in the soil. Water less often in winter and do not feed. It is natural for older leaves to become yellow and these should be removed promptly.

MEDIA

In standard pots, use an all-purpose potting mix. It is also easily grown in hydroculture.

OVERALL RATING	7.0
Removal of chemical vapours	
Ease of growth and maintenance	
Resistance to insect infestation	
Transpiration rate	

RED EMERALD PHILODENDRON

(Philodendron erubescens)

Introduced as a houseplant around 1900, the red emerald is one of the most common vining types. Its leaves are rather long and narrow with yellow veins. It is a hybrid that is sought for its striking burgundy-red leaves. It can be propagated by taking cuttings at a joint and rooting in moist potting mix.

As with all philodendrons, it is easy to care for, preferring warmth and humidity. However, it does need to be staked or given support for climbing. Water-absorbent poles such as those made from wire and sphagnum moss are ideal. It has added environmental value, as it is a leader among the philodendrons in removing indoor air pollutants. Vining philodendrons, such as *P. erubescens*, are among the easiest houseplants to maintain.

FAMILY

Araceae (arum).

ORIGIN

South America.

LIGHT

Semi-shade to shade.

TEMPERATURE

Ideally, 16–21°C (60–70°F). Never allow the temperature to drop below 13°C (55°F) or to rise above 24°C (75°F).

PESTS AND PROBLEMS

Occasionally aphids, scale insects and mealybugs. Root rot from cold, wet soil.

CARE

Keep soil evenly moist, but not soggy during its growth period. Water less in winter. Apply a liquid fertilizer at half-strength during its growing season. Mist often. Wipe leaves occasionally with a damp cloth.

MEDIA

Grows equally well in soil or hydroculture. Less frequent watering is needed in hydroculture.

OVERALL RATING   7.0

Removal of chemical vapours	■ ■ ■ ■ ■ ■
Ease of growth and maintenance	■ ■ ■ ■ ■ ■ ■
Resistance to insect infestation	■ ■ ■ ■ ■
Transpiration rate	■ ■ ■ ■

SYNGONIUM

(*Syngonium podophyllum*)

Syngoniums are attractive plants whose ease of growth and maintenance and resistance to insect infestation make them a popular choice for home or office. There are 30 distinct cultivars of *Syngonium podophyllum* and it is known by a variety of common names (arrowhead vine, white butterfly or goosefoot plant). Often mistaken for its relative the philodendron, the arrowhead vine features green-white or green-silver variegated leaves. Its special characteristic is that its young leaves are long and arrow-shaped. With age, however, the leaves evolve into three- to five-lobed stars. Multiple-lobed leaves and arrow-shaped leaves appear on the same plant.

Syngoniums love humidity and are happy with frequent misting. Wipe leaves occasionally with a damp cloth to remove dust. They do well in hanging baskets, but must be rotated to ensure even growth. Pinch back the shoots regularly to obtain a thick, bushy appearance. Grown in hydroculture, they rarely need repotting.

FAMILY

Araceae (arum).

ORIGIN

Central America.

LIGHT

Semi-sun to shade.

TEMPERATURE

16–24°C (60–75°F).

PESTS AND PROBLEMS

Rarely scale insects, aphids, spider mites and mealybugs. Attacks usually occur when the air is too dry.

CARE

Feed regularly, except winter, with a complete fertilizer solution. Keep the soil evenly moist (but not soggy) from spring to autumn. Allow the top soil to dry between waterings in winter. Mist often.

MEDIA

Syngoniums grow equally well in potting mix or hydroculture.

OVERALL RATING	7.0
Removal of chemical vapours	
Ease of growth and maintenance	
Resistance to insect infestation	
Transpiration rate	

DUMB CANE

(*Dieffenbachia "Exotica Compacta"*)

The genus *Dieffenbachia* was named in 1830 in honour of the German botanist, J. F. Dieffenbach, who was the gardener at the Schönbrunn Palace in Vienna. It derives its common name, dumb cane, from the calcium oxalate in its sap. Chewing any part of the plant causes temporary numbness of the tongue and vocal chords.

D. "Exotica" is one of the most strikingly beautiful foliage plants and quickly became the most popular of the species. The "Compacta" is the dwarf variety and features wide, blotched green and white (cream) leaves. Variegated leaves will lose their colour if there is not enough light. It usually grows to a maximum height of about 0.6 m (2 ft). Its broad, lance-shaped leaves spread outwards from unbranched stems and arch downward, making it one of the most showy foliage plants. Its main drawbacks are fast growth and a tendency to grow towards a light source. If the plant becomes too large or has lost leaves, it can be cut back. It will quickly put out new growth. Its large leaf surface helps to make it an effective plant for removing indoor air contaminants.

FAMILY

Araceae (arum).

ORIGIN

Tropical Central and South America.

LIGHT

Semi-sun to semi-shade.

TEMPERATURE

16–27°C (60–80°F); will tolerate temperatures as low as 9°C (48°F) for short periods.

PESTS AND PROBLEMS

Spider mites, aphids, and thrips. Root rot from overwatering.

CARE

Keep moist with soft, tepid water. Water more sparingly in winter. Apply diluted liquid fertilizer from March to August. Mist the leaves often. Avoid draughs.

MEDIA

When grown in soil, it prefers peat mixes or compost of loam, peat, leaf-mould and sand. It thrives in hydroculture.

WARNING

All parts of the plant are poisonous.

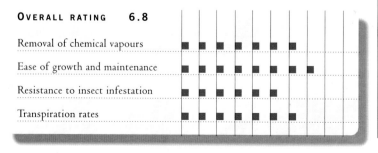

OVERALL RATING	6.8
Removal of chemical vapours	
Ease of growth and maintenance	
Resistance to insect infestation	
Transpiration rates	

PARLOUR PALM

(Chamaedorea elegans)

The parlour palm has been valued as a houseplant since Victorian times and remains equally popular today. Nowadays it is more often sold in a cluster than as a single plant. The parlour palm, also known as *Neanthe bella*, has a more delicate appearance than most palms. Although it can reach a height of 1.8 m (6 ft), its average height is closer to 1 m (3 ft). The parlour palm has a small, stiff trunk that produces light-green fronds about 20 cm (8 in) long. It is a slow grower. Tolerant of the low light and lack of humidity found in most buildings, it is easy to maintain. In fact, few plants can withstand more neglect.

The parlour palm begins to bloom before reaching maturity. If happy with its placement and growing conditions, it can produce flowers all year round. However, it is best to cut the flowers off before they unfold to prevent any problems with pollen. Do not prune; this plant has a terminal bud or single point of growth.

FAMILY

Arecaceae (palm).

ORIGIN

Mexico and Guatemala.

LIGHT

Semi-sun to semi-shade.

TEMPERATURE

20–27°C (68–80°F); slightly cooler in winter.

PESTS AND PROBLEMS

Spider mites. Too much water will cause root rot.

CARE

Keep roots moist. Water frequently during the growing season from March to September. Feed with a weak solution of fertilizer every three to four weeks. Mist often.

MEDIA

Any of the palms may be grown in potting mix or hydroculture.

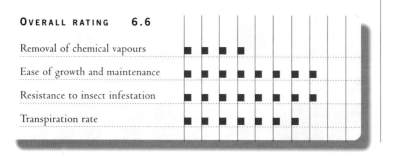

OVERALL RATING   6.6

Removal of chemical vapours

Ease of growth and maintenance

Resistance to insect infestation

Transpiration rate

WEEPING FIG

(Ficus benjamina)

These popular trees are common in homes, shopping centres and the lobbies and atriums of many public buildings. The biggest drawback is their dislike of being moved. Once happy, it is easy to grow. This ficus is excellent for the removal of indoor air pollutants, especially formaldehyde.

There are bright to dark-green leaved and variegated leaved species commonly available. Its common name is derived from its gracefully drooping branches. There are three types: the standard tree, bush (several stems emerge from one pot) and the braid (which consists of two or three entwined trunks).

Leaf drop is common until it adjusts to its new environment. Older leaves naturally turn yellow and drop in the winter. Once acclimatized to its environment, it should thrive for years. An underplanting of pothos or ivy adds to its visual impact and increases the air-cleaning effect.

FAMILY
Moraceae (fig).

ORIGIN
Tropics and subtropics.

LIGHT
Full sun to semi-sun.

TEMPERATURE
Day: 16–24°C (60–75°F); night: 13–20°C (55–68°F).

PESTS AND PROBLEMS
Scale insects and mealybugs. Root rot if overwatered.

CARE
Keep soil moist, but not soggy. Feed every two weeks during summer. It prefers to be potbound, so yearly repotting is not necessary.

MEDIA
Thrives exceptionally well in hydroculture or sub-irrigation. Growing in an all-purpose potting mix requires more care.

OVERALL RATING   6.5

Removal of chemical vapours	■ ■ ■ ■ ■ ■ ■
Ease of growth and maintenance	■ ■ ■ ■ ■ ■
Resistance to insect infestation	■ ■ ■ ■
Transpiration rate	■ ■ ■

SCHEFFLERA
(*Brassaia actinophylla*)

Commonly known as the umbrella tree, this stately plant reaches a height of 2.5 to 3.1 m (8 – 10 ft) indoors. A smaller species, *Schefflera arboricola*, grows to only about 1.2 m (4 ft) and has recently become available in variegated form. At one time, schefflera was the most favoured big indoor plant. It is somewhat less popular today as other plants have taken its place. Yet it is one of the easiest large plants to grow. Consideration to its placement should be given before purchase.

Schefflera has long stems with 7 to 16 polished leaves, each up to 30 cm (12 in) long. Their formation resembles the ribs of an umbrella and, hence, the plant's common name. To reduce the height of the larger schefflera, prune the main stems back to a node (the point at which leaves join the stem).

This plant is excellent for the novice indoor gardener or those who tend to neglect their plants. Its major drawback is its tendency to attract pests. Check to make sure the plant is pest-free at time of purchase, and mist often to reduce the risk of insect infestation.

FAMILY

Araliaceae (aralia).

ORIGIN

Northeastern Australia, Java, Taiwan, New Guinea and New Zealand.

LIGHT

Semi-shade.

TEMPERATURE

18–24°C (65–75°F); do not allow to drop below 13°C (55°F).

PESTS AND PROBLEMS

Aphids, spider mites, mealybugs and scale insects, especially if the air is too dry.

CARE

Water thoroughly, allowing the soil to dry slightly between waterings. Water less in autumn and winter. Feed with dilute water-soluble fertilizer every two weeks in spring and summer and once a month in autumn and winter. Mist often.

MEDIA

Grows exceptionally well in hydroculture. In standard containers, use commercial all-purpose potting mix.

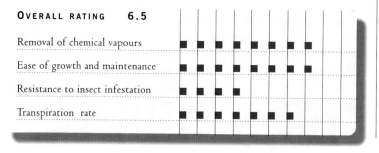

OVERALL RATING	6.5
Removal of chemical vapours	
Ease of growth and maintenance	
Resistance to insect infestation	
Transpiration rate	

WAX BEGONIA

(Begonia semperflorens)

Begonias are named for M. Michael Begon, a 17th-century French-Canadian naturalist. *B. semperflorens* (meaning ever-blooming) has fine, fibrous root systems that produce many compact, fleshy stems topped with waxy rounded leaves. A healthy plant will bloom throughout the year, producing flowers ranging from white to pink, red, orange, yellow, or any combination of these. There are many varieties available that can provide a profusion of colours.

These begonias are succulents and as such are sensitive to excessive watering. They also prefer as much bright light as possible.

Begonias are not especially difficult to grow and provide colour accents when grouped with foliage plants. If leaves become pale, move to a less sunny location. If leaves turn brown at the edges, this may indicate that the air is too dry.

FAMILY

Begoniaceae (begonia).

ORIGIN

Brazil.

LIGHT

Full sun to semi-sun.

TEMPERATURE

16–24°C (60–75°F).

PESTS AND PROBLEMS

Rarely attacked by pests. Fungal disease or mildew may occur if conditions are too damp or if air circulation is insufficient.

CARE

Provide a complete fertilizer every two weeks throughout the year. Allow soil to dry slightly between waterings. Begonias are very sensitive to overwatering. To prevent legginess and to produce stronger blooms, pinch back young plants. Do not mist; damp leaves encourage mildew spores.

MEDIA

Use a loose potting mix that drains well.

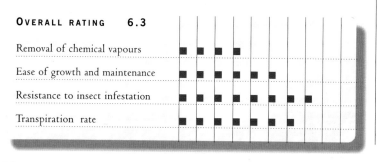

OVERALL RATING	6.3								
Removal of chemical vapours									
Ease of growth and maintenance									
Resistance to insect infestation									
Transpiration rate									

LACY TREE PHILODENDRON

(Philodendron selloum)

Of the self-heading or bushy-type philodendrons, the lacy tree is the most popular and the best suited for indoor culture. It is available in dwarf form or in hybrid varieties. It can tolerate a drier atmosphere and much lower lighting levels than most other philodendrons. With proper care, this philodendron can be maintained for years. However, as the plant matures, it will need space to spread.

Most often seen in atriums or lobbies of public buildings, the lacy tree philodendron can have a dramatic effect in a large room with high ceilings.

The lacy tree produces large, deeply cut leaves. As the plant matures, the cuts become more pronounced and cause the leaves to ruffle. Bright light and adequate warmth and moisture will cause it to grow full, short and strong. To slow its growth, cut back on the amount of fertilizer and keep it somewhat potbound.

FAMILY

Araceae (arum).

ORIGIN

South America.

LIGHT

Semi-shade.

TEMPERATURE

Ideally, 16–21°C (60–70°F). Never allow the temperature to drop below 13°C (55°F) or rise above 24°C (75°F).

PESTS AND PROBLEMS

Occasionally aphids, scale insects and mealybugs. Root rot from cold, wet soil.

CARE

Keep soil evenly moist, but not soggy during its growing season. Water less in winter. Apply a half-strength fertilizer during the growth period only. Mist often. Occasionally wipe leaves with a damp cloth or sponge.

MEDIA

Use an all-purpose potting mix. It grows well in hydroponics, which requires a less frequent watering schedule.

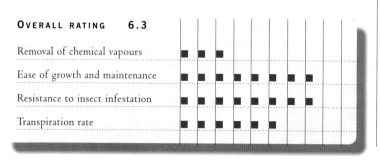

OVERALL RATING 6.3

	Rating
Removal of chemical vapours	
Ease of growth and maintenance	
Resistance to insect infestation	
Transpiration rate	

HEART-LEAF PHILODENDRON

(*Philodendron oxycardium*)

This plant is easily recognized by its heart-shaped leaves. Also known as *Philodendron scandens*, this is probably the most common of all philodendrons. It is a climber and can reach a height of 2 m (6 ft). It is one of the most popular houseplants, largely because of its tolerance to low-light conditions. Introduced as a house-plant around 1850, it is composed of many glossy, dark-green leaves. These are heart-shaped and taper to a sharp point.

Heart-leaf philodendron is one of the easiest philodendrons to grow. To give it a more bushy appearance, regularly pinch out some of its growing tips. It will benefit greatly from frequent misting.

It can be propagated by taking pieces of stem with leaves attached and rooting in moist potting mixture. Because it is a slow grower, it is excellent in a hanging basket. Fairly resistant to insects, this plant should always be included in any mixed display of houseplants.

FAMILY

Araceae (arum).

ORIGIN

South America.

LIGHT

Semi-shade to shade.

TEMPERATURE

Ideally, 16–21°C (60–70°F). Never allow the temperature to drop below 13°C (55°F) or rise above 24°C (75°F).

PESTS AND PROBLEMS

Aphids, mealybugs and scale insects. Root rot from too wet and cold conditions.

CARE

Feed every two weeks except in winter. Large plants need full-strength fertilizer; a weak solution is best for smaller plants. Keep the soil evenly moist, but water less frequently in winter. Mist often. Clean leaves occasionally with a damp cloth or sponge.

MEDIA

Grows well in soil or hydroculture. Regardless of growing medium, this climber needs a support.

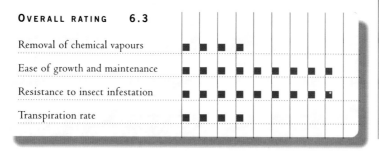

OVERALL RATING	6.3
Removal of chemical vapours	
Ease of growth and maintenance	
Resistance to insect infestation	
Transpiration rate	

Snake plant
(*Sansevieria trifasciata*)

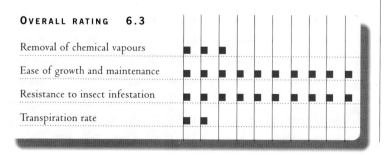

The snake plant presents an interesting contrast when grouped with other plants. It is easy to grow and tolerates a great deal of neglect. Its ease of growth and resistance to insects make it a good "starter" plant for those new to growing houseplants.

Commonly, though unkindly, referred to as the "mother-in-law's tongue", the snake plant is almost indestructible.

There are about 70 species, but *Sansevieria trifasciata* is the most common. It features stiff, spear-like leaves that stand rigidly upright; usually 0.6 to 1.2m (2 – 4 ft) in length and approximately 5 cm (2 in) wide. They occasionally bloom, sending forth small, greenish-white, fragrant flowers. Any flowers should be removed as they release a sticky, honey-like substance.

The snake plant differs from most houseplants in that it produces oxygen and removes carbon dioxide at night. Because they are so easy to grow, always include them in any mixture of houseplants.

FAMILY

Agavaceae (agave).

ORIGIN

Tropical West Africa, India.

LIGHT

Semi-sun, semi-shade or shade.

TEMPERATURE

18–27°C (65–80°F).

PESTS AND PROBLEMS

Rarely attacked by insects. Root rot from overwatering is the main risk.

CARE

Water sparingly. Let the soil dry between waterings. Give a dilute solution of liquid fertilizer about once a month.

MEDIA

Grows in soil, but needs yearly repotting. In hydroculture, it can grow for years without repotting.

OVERALL RATING	6.3
Removal of chemical vapours	
Ease of growth and maintenance	
Resistance to insect infestation	
Transpiration rate	

DUMB CANE

(*Dieffenbachia camilla*)

This is a popular plant that is highly valued for its attractive pattern and colour. The foliage often provides as much colour as plants in bloom and its broad leaves help to add moisture (through transpiration) to the surrounding air. Its foliage is usually green with white or yellow marbled patterns.

All species of dieffenbachia are commonly called dumb cane (see also Dieffenbachia "Exotica Compacta", p.78) because their sap contains calcium oxalate. Biting any part of the plant will cause the throat to swell and loss of speech can last for several days.

D. camilla is adaptable to most home and office environments, but prefers bright, filtered light as occurs near a window. Variegated leaves lose their colour in too dark a setting. The dwarf variety reaches only about 0.6 m (2 ft), and thus is best suited for home use.

FAMILY

Araceae (arum).

ORIGIN

Colombia, Venezuela and Ecuador.

LIGHT

Semi-sun to semi-shade.

TEMPERATURE

16–29°C (60–85°F); will tolerate temperatures as low as 8°C (46°F) for short periods, but will drop leaves if left cold too long.

PESTS AND PROBLEMS

Spider mites, aphids, thrips and mealybugs.

CARE

Keep moist with soft, tepid water. In winter water more sparingly. Use diluted liquid fertilizer from March to August. Mist often. This plant does not tolerate draughts.

MEDIA

When using soil, make up a mixture of three parts leaf-mould to one part ordinary soil. Dieffenbachia thrives equally well in hydroculture.

WARNING:

All parts of the plant are poisonous.

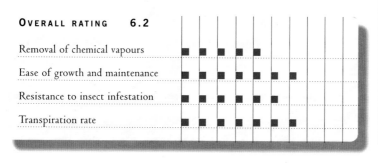

OVERALL RATING	6.2
Removal of chemical vapours	
Ease of growth and maintenance	
Resistance to insect infestation	
Transpiration rate	

ELEPHANT EAR PHILODENDRON

(Philodendron domesticum or Philodendron tuxla)

Also known as spade-leaf philodendron and sometimes sold as *Philodendron hastatum*, this philodendron derives its common name from its long, arrow-shaped leaves that resemble the ears of elephants. It is easy to grow and fairly resistant to insects. As with any plant originating in the tropics, it prefers warmth, humidity and indirect light.

At maturity, the leaves are about 17 cm (7 in) long and 10 cm (4 in) across at the widest point. It can produce yellowish-white flowers, but this is rare in cultivation. This species is somewhat slower growing than other philodendrons.

This philodendron is not a climber, but a vining type. It must be supported by some means. Water-absorbent supports are best, for they help give the plant moisture. Slabs of redwood bark or wire and sphagnum moss poles work well. This attractive display plant is a popular choice in the home as well as in commercial settings.

FAMILY

Araceae (arum).

ORIGIN

Brazil.

LIGHT

Shade or semi-shade.

TEMPERATURE

Ideally, 16–21°C (60–70°F). Never allow the temperature to drop below 13°C (55°F) or rise above 24°C (75°F).

PESTS AND PROBLEMS

Aphids, scale insects and mealybugs. Root rot from wet, cold soil.

CARE

Keep soil evenly moist, but not soggy during growing season. Water less often in winter. Apply a liquid fertilizer at half-strength throughout the year. Mist often. Clean leaves occasionally by wiping with a damp cloth.

MEDIA

Grows equally well in soil or hydroculture. However, less frequent watering is required in hydroculture.

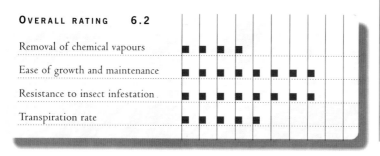

OVERALL RATING	6.2
Removal of chemical vapours	■ ■ ■ ■
Ease of growth and maintenance	■ ■ ■ ■ ■ ■ ■
Resistance to insect infestation	■ ■ ■ ■ ■
Transpiration rate	■ ■ ■ ■

NORFOLK ISLAND PINE

(*Araucaria heterophylla*)

The Norfolk Island pine is an attractive evergreen conifer, discovered by Captain Cook and botanist Sir Joseph Banks. There are more than 15 known varieties. However, only the *heterophylla* is acceptable for the indoor environment. Having an appearance of a true pine tree, its tiered branches carry soft needles.

New layers of needles are bright green and turn darker with age. In its native habitat it can grow to nearly 61 m (200 ft). However, indoors its maximum height is likely to be about 3 m (10 ft). This plant is a slow grower, generally adding one tier of branches per growing season. It makes an excellent accent plant.

The Norfolk Island pine is not difficult to grow. However, if there is needle drop or branches begin to droop, conditions are probably too warm or it is receiving too much water in the winter. The Norfolk Island pine often serves as a miniature Christmas tree. However, care should be taken not to break fragile branches when hanging decorations from them.

FAMILY

Pinaceae (pine).

ORIGIN

Norfolk Island (South Pacific).

LIGHT

Full sun to semi-shade.

TEMPERATURE

18–22°C (64–72°F). In winter keep cool, but not below 5°C (41°F).

PESTS AND PROBLEMS

Aphids and mealybugs.

CARE

During the most active growing period, March to August, keep moderately damp using only soft water. Water sparingly in winter. Feed with a weak concentration of fertilizer during the growing season. Mist often.

MEDIA

Will grow in standard containers, hydroculture or sub-irrigation.

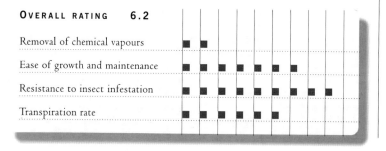

OVERALL RATING	6.2								
Removal of chemical vapours	■	■							
Ease of growth and maintenance	■	■	■	■	■	■			
Resistance to insect infestation	■	■	■	■	■	■	■	■	
Transpiration rate	■	■	■	■	■				

KING OF HEARTS

(Homalomena wallisii)

The King of Hearts is an attractive plant, but somewhat difficult to maintain. As stronger cultivars are developed, it will probably become more popular. It is among the best plants tested for the removal of ammonia from the air.

There are about 130 species of *Homalomena*. However, only *H. wallisii* is frequently cultivated for indoor use. This genus is sometimes confused with *Schismatoglottis*, although it is not related. The King of Hearts is related to the philodendron. It produces showy foliage. It has dark, olive-green, oval-shaped leaves sprinkled with areas of silver or cream. The leaves reach maturity at about 20 cm (8 in) in length, but are slow growing. Because it is rather temperamental, it is not commonly used in the home environment. However, the professional interior plantscape industry uses the plant for its handsome foliage.

FAMILY

Araceae (arum).

ORIGIN

Tropical regions of Asia and the Americas.

LIGHT

Semi-shade to shade.

TEMPERATURE

16–24°C (60–75°F). Avoid draughts.

PESTS AND PROBLEMS

Spider mites in too warm and dry a location.

CARE

Keep evenly moist. Use room-temperature soft water or rainwater, if possible. Provide a weak solution of liquid fertilizer regularly from spring to autumn.

MEDIA

Use a standard commercial potting mix and provide good drainage.

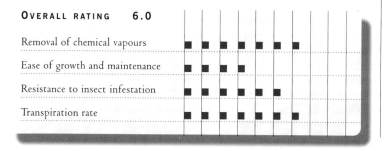

OVERALL RATING	6.0
Removal of chemical vapours	
Ease of growth and maintenance	
Resistance to insect infestation	
Transpiration rate	

PRAYER PLANT

(*Maranta leuconeura* "Kerchoveana")

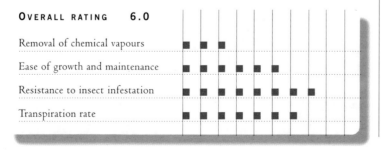

The prayer plant, with its distinctive markings and habit of folding its leaves, is an interesting indoor specimen. It is not often found in offices, but could make a nice conversation piece on a desk. Its common name is derived from the way its leaves turn upwards as dusk approaches, giving the appearance of praying hands. Actually, this is the plant's method of conserving moisture.

M. leuconeura is a small, bushy plant with broad, light-green leaves decorated with rows of brown to dark-green spots on both sides of its midrib. These plants naturally grow low, reaching a height of only 20 to 30 cm (8 – 12 in). They spread out as they mature. There are several varieties of *Maranta*, but the prayer plant is the easiest to grow. If the prayer plant regularly opens its leaves during the day and closes them at night, you can be fairly confident that it is happy with its surroundings.

FAMILY

Marantaceae (arrowroot).

ORIGIN

South America.

LIGHT

Semi-sun to semi-shade.

TEMPERATURE

Day: 21–27°C (70–80°F); night: 16–21°C (60–70°F).

PESTS AND PROBLEMS

Spider mites and mealybugs in dry, centrally heated air. Brown leaf edges from too cool a location.

CARE

Keep evenly moist, but water less often in winter. Feed every two weeks in spring and summer. Mist frequently. Snip off old, ragged leaves.

MEDIA

Grows in standard all-purpose potting mix or hydroculture.

OVERALL RATING	6.0
Removal of chemical vapours	
Ease of growth and maintenance	
Resistance to insect infestation	
Transpiration rate	

Dwarf Banana

(*Musa cavendishii*)

The dwarf banana, reaching a height of only 0.6 to 1.5 m (2 – 5 ft), is relatively new in the houseplant world. If you have a sun lounge or a sunny window location and want a tropical look, then you might try the dwarf banana. Its broad, shiny, exotic-looking leaves give any interior decor a tropical accent. However, its need for light, warmth and humidity makes it difficult to maintain. It is rare for the banana to produce fruit in the indoor environment, chiefly due to a lack of sufficient light. Its leaves also split easily and can become ragged looking. Realistically, it will probably not look good for more than a year or two even under ideal conditions.

Its large leaves cause it to transpire moisture into the air at a prodigious rate. High transpiration rates are desirable in the dry atmosphere of centrally heated homes in winter.

FAMILY

Musaceae (banana).

ORIGIN

Tropical Asia and Western Pacific.

LIGHT

Full sun to semi-sun.

TEMPERATURE

Ideally, 18–24°C (65–75°F), but will survive in temperatures as low as 10°C (50°F) for short periods.

PESTS AND PROBLEMS

Spider mites and mealybugs.

CARE

Keep constantly moist, but do not let water stand in the saucer. Provide fertilizer with every watering, except in winter.

MEDIA

Pot in a planter 30 cm (12-in) in diameter using equal parts potting mix and peat moss. Needs less frequent watering and repotting in hydroculture.

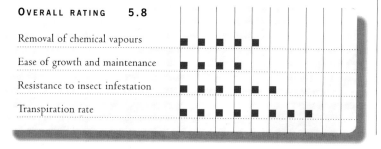

OVERALL RATING	5.8								
Removal of chemical vapours									
Ease of growth and maintenance									
Resistance to insect infestation									
Transpiration rate									

CHRISTMAS AND EASTER CACTUS

(*Schlumbergera bridgesii; Schlumbergera rhipsalidopsis*)

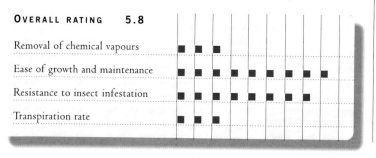

These cacti are delightful and fascinating houseplants. The Christmas cactus has bright green, arched branches with flattened joints about every 4 cm (1½ in).

The branches droop, especially when in bloom. Buds usually set and are in full bloom in December. Native species are found in the Orgel Mountains near Rio de Janeiro. The hybrids on the market today are a cross between *Zygocactus truncatus* and *Schlumbergera russeliana*. These hybrids are available in white, pink, red, purple-red, violet and yellow. Its profusion of bright blooms lasts for several weeks.

The Easter cactus is similar in appearance but droops less and blooms in the spring.

Both Christmas and Easter forms have the unusual property of removing carbon dioxide and releasing oxygen at night – the opposite of most plants. They can become quite large and often survive for many years. Propagation is quite easily accomplished by rooting stem cuttings.

FAMILY

Cactaceae (cactus).

ORIGIN

Brazil.

LIGHT.

Semi-sun.

TEMPERATURE

18–22°C (64–72°F).

PESTS AND PROBLEMS

Although highly resistant to insect infestation, under stress it may be attacked by mealybugs and spider mites. Buds may drop if there is a change in environmental conditions once the buds are set.

CARE

Water until the soil is moist and allow to dry between waterings. Feed every two weeks in summer, then reduce water and fertilizer so that the leaves will mature. Mist frequently.

MEDIA

A mix of 1 part potting mix, 2 parts leaf mould and 1 part perlite is ideal.

OVERALL RATING	5.8
Removal of chemical vapours	■ ■ ■
Ease of growth and maintenance	■ ■ ■ ■ ■ ■ ■ ■
Resistance to insect infestation	■ ■ ■ ■ ■ ■
Transpiration rate	■ ■ ■

OAKLEAF IVY

(*Cissus rhombifolia* "Ellen Danika")

The oakleaf ivy is an attractive vining plant. This cultivar is more compact than other varieties, but still requires pruning to encourage a bushy appearance. Its reddish tint is best seen from a hanging basket.

"Ellen Danika" is currently the most popular cultivar and is widely used in public buildings. It is most often found in hanging baskets and is quite easy to grow and maintain. This cultivar is distinguished by deeply lobed leaves that resemble an oak leaf, hence its common name. It is more compact than other varieties and its green leaves sometimes have reddish hairs. The oakleaf ivy is a graceful and rapidly growing plant. To prevent it from becoming straggly, pinch off growing tips. "Ellen Danika" makes a good office plant as it can withstand some neglect.

If sufficient space is available, try training oakleaf ivy on a trellis. The greater leaf surface allows it to purify air more effectively. Hydroculture is the preferred method of growing for trellis-trained plants, as less frequent watering is required.

FAMILY

Vitaceae (grape).

ORIGIN

Mexico to Colombia.

LIGHT

Semi-sun to semi-shade.

TEMPERATURE

Day: 18–24°C (65–75°F); night: 13–18°C (55–65°F).

PESTS AND PROBLEMS

May suffer from spider mites in too warm a location and from fungal infections if the soil is too wet, especially in winter.

CARE

Water thoroughly, then let the top layer of soil dry between waterings. Provide weak fertilizer with each watering from March to August.

MEDIA

Use an all-purpose potting mix. Oakleaf ivy also performs well in hydroculture.

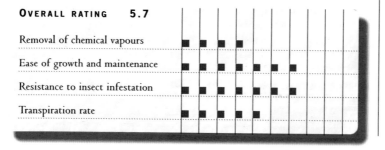

OVERALL RATING   5.7

Removal of chemical vapours

Ease of growth and maintenance

Resistance to insect infestation

Transpiration rate

LILY TURF

(Liriope spicata)

Most often grown outdoors as edging for borders or in rock gardens, lily turf also makes an interesting and unusual indoor houseplant. It can be grown as an individual houseplant, but it is shown to best advantage as border grass in a large display planting. Lily turf is used extensively by commercial interior plantscapers. Its grassy and arching evergreen leaves reach 15 to 45 cm (6 – 18 in) at maturity and may be dark green or variegated. The mature plant reaches a height of about 30 cm (1 ft). It produces small, 30-cm (1-ft) spikes of white or lavender flowers in summer.

Lily turf spreads by underground runners, which are easily divided at almost any time of year. It is particularly effective for removing ammonia from the air.

FAMILY

Liliaceae (lily).

ORIGIN

China and Japan.

LIGHT

Semi-sun to semi-shade.

TEMPERATURE

16–24°C (60–75°F).

PESTS AND PROBLEMS

Scale insects and aphids in air that is too dry.

CARE

A semi-aquatic plant, lily turf requires constantly moist soil. Feed monthly with fertilizer in spring, summer and autumn.

MEDIA

Use a loose-mix potting mix to provide good drainage. When grown in hydroculture, less frequent watering is required.

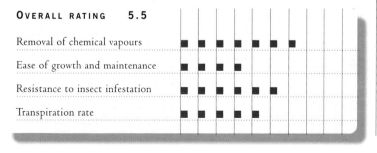

OVERALL RATING   5.5

Removal of chemical vapours

Ease of growth and maintenance

Resistance to insect infestation

Transpiration rate

DENDROBIUM ORCHID

(*Dendrobium* sp.)

The genus name comes from the Greek word meaning "life in a tree", indicating that most, but not all, are epiphytic. Interestingly, desert plants, such as cactus, and epiphytic bromeliads and orchids from the jungle absorb carbon dioxide and release oxygen at night, the opposite of most plants. Hybrid orchids are probably best for beginners as they are more tolerant of typical home environments. When environmental conditions are met, the dendrobium orchid puts forth beautiful exotic blooms. The flowers are long-lasting and worth the extra effort these plants require.

Specific growth requirements for each species should be determined at the time of purchase. To produce flowers, some species require cool temperatures in the autumn, some want a dry period and still others need a cool and dry period. The flowers usually bloom in clusters or in a row on drooping canes. Flowers can last a week or up to several months, depending upon the species. Dendrobiums are moderately effective at removing alcohols, acetone, formaldehyde and chloroform from the atmosphere.

FAMILY

Orchidaceae (orchid).

ORIGIN

Australia, China, India, Indonesia, Japan, Korea, New Zealand.

LIGHT

Semi-sun.

TEMPERATURE

Day: 16–24°C (60–75°F); night: 13–18°C (55–65°F).

PESTS AND PROBLEMS

Overwatering can cause fungal infection. Scale insects and spider mites may occur in air that is too dry.

CARE

Water generously in spring and summer. In winter water just enough to keep the bulbs from shrivelling and do not feed. Mist often, especially in summer.

MEDIA

Use commercially prepared orchid mix or decayed oak leaves, Spanish moss or sphagnum moss.

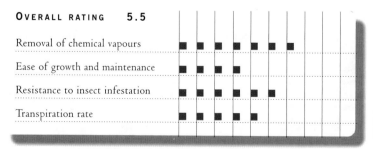

OVERALL RATING   5.5

Removal of chemical vapours	
Ease of growth and maintenance	
Resistance to insect infestation	
Transpiration rate	

SPIDER PLANT

(*Chlorophytum comosum "Vittatum"*)

Also known as the airplane plant, the spider plant was given world-wide attention in 1984 when NASA first released research findings showing its ability to remove indoor air pollutants. The cultivar "Vittatum" (meaning white-striped leaves) is the most common form of spider plant. It produces green leaves with a broad centre stripe of yellow or cream. These are 15 to 30 cm (6 – 12 in) long. It sends up slender, arching shoots that yield small white flowers at virtually any time of year. These flowers are quickly followed by airborne plantlets. The plantlets can be removed for propagation or left on the parent plant. A plant with many plantlets has a full look that is perfect for hanging baskets. The basket should be rotated periodically to achieve even growth.

FAMILY
Liliaceae (lily).

ORIGIN
South Africa.

LIGHT
Semi-sun to semi-shade.

TEMPERATURE
Day: 18–24°C (65–75°F); night: 13–18°C (55–65°F).

PESTS AND PROBLEMS
Aphids, scale insects and mealybugs may occur in too dry a location

CARE
Keep evenly moist, but allow the soil to dry slightly between waterings. Feed regularly in spring and summer, but less in autumn and winter.

MEDIA
Grows well in hydroculture or all-purpose potting mix.

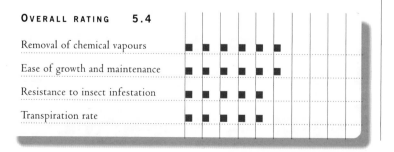

OVERALL RATING   5.4

Removal of chemical vapours	
Ease of growth and maintenance	
Resistance to insect infestation	
Transpiration rate	

CHINESE EVERGREEN

(*Aglaonema crispum* "Silver Queen")

The Chinese evergreen is currently enjoying widespread popularity in the home and in public buildings. It is extremely tolerant of low light conditions, but suffers in temperatures below 13°C (55°F). The light green and silvery leaves of the "Silver Queen" variety stand out when grouped with other plants having plain dark green foliage.

The "Silver Queen" has attractive, 15 to 30 cm (6 – 12-in), grey-green, lance-shaped leaves marked with silver on shallow-rooted short stalks. Under suitable conditions, it blooms in late summer or early autumn. After flowering, the Chinese evergreen produces red berries, which are poisonous. Although somewhat slow growing, these plants can reach a height and width of about 0.9 m (3 ft).

Chinese evergreen's most notable quality is its ability to grow in dimly lit areas. This ability, added to its showy foliage, ensures its enduring popularity as a houseplant. It also has the capacity to increase its rate of removal of toxins from the atmosphere with increasing exposure.

FAMILY

Araceae (arum).

ORIGIN

Southeast Asia.

LIGHT

Semi-shade to shade.

TEMPERATURE

16–21°C (60–70°F). This plant cannot tolerate cold conditions.

PESTS AND PROBLEMS

Spider mites, scale insects, mealybugs and aphids may occur in dry indoor air.

CARE

Keep moist with soft, tepid water during active growth season, less in winter. Feed every two weeks with diluted liquid fertilizer. Avoid misting, which causes leaf spots.

MEDIA

Use an all-purpose potting mix. It will also grow in soil-less media.

WARNING

This plant contains substances that irritate skin and mucous membranes. The berries are poisonous. They can be snipped off with scissors.

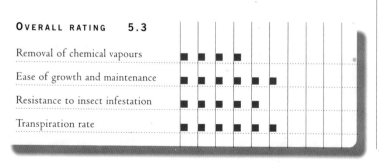

OVERALL RATING	5.3
Removal of chemical vapours	
Ease of growth and maintenance	
Resistance to insect infestation	
Transpiration rate	

ANTHURIUM

(Anthurium andraeanum)

There are approximately 600 species of anthuriums, but only three varieties are suitable for growing in the home. The most popular cultivar is the "Lady Jane". Anthuriums originated in the tropics and therefore prefer warm and humid conditions, which are often difficult to achieve indoors. Belonging to the same family as the peace lily, anthuriums are also sought for their display of spathes set against their dark green foliage. Unlike the peace lily, however, their spathes come in a variety of colours including white, pink, red and coral. The spathe lasts for weeks, but the flower should be cut out to prevent the release of pollen.

Anthuriums are not easy plants to grow. They are demanding regarding their preferred light and temperature. They love humidity and do not do well in the dry air of most homes and offices in winter. In commercial situations, they are usually removed after their spathes have peaked. However, if their needs can be met, their beautiful foliage and colourful spathes make the extra effort worthwhile.

FAMILY

Araceae (arum).

ORIGIN

Colombia.

LIGHT

Semi-sun.

TEMPERATURE

18–24°C (65–75°F).

PESTS AND PROBLEMS

Spider mites may be a problem in a dry environment. The fungus botrytis is a risk if conditions are too cold or damp.

CARE

Keep consistently damp from spring to autumn, but water less in winter. Use soft, tepid water. Feed once a week with diluted liquid fertilizer from March to September. Use a damp sponge or brush to clean the leaves. Do not mist or the leaves will develop brown spots.

MEDIA

For standard containers or sub-irrigation, use equal parts of peat, sphagnum moss and leaf mould. Anthuriums may also be grown using hydroculture techniques.

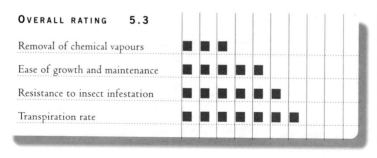

OVERALL RATING   5.3

Removal of chemical vapours

Ease of growth and maintenance

Resistance to insect infestation

Transpiration rate

CROTON

(Codiaeum variegatum pictum)

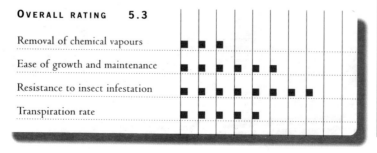

The many-coloured croton can brighten and add contrast to a grouping of foliage plants. Croton is also commonly known as Joseph's Coat for the biblical reference to Joseph's coat of many colours. Its leaves grow from a single stem or trunk and are leathery and oak-like and come in various combinations of yellow, orange, red, green and purple-red. New leaves are green and change colour as they mature. Mature leaves have splotches, marginal colouring and veins that often show contrasting colours. Without enough light, however, the colouring will fade. The plant can reach a height of 0.6 to 1.2 m (2 – 4 ft).

Although temperamental until all of its environmental needs are met, the croton's brilliantly coloured foliage makes the extra effort worthwhile. Given lots of light, warmth and humidity – it will probably enjoy a sunny spot near a window – the croton can be a showpiece.

FAMILY

Euphorbiaceae (spurge).

ORIGIN

Sri Lanka, Malaya and southern India.

LIGHT

Full sun to semi-shade.

TEMPERATURE

Day: 24–27°C (75–80°F); night: 18–21°C (65–70°F). Avoid sudden changes in temperature.

PESTS AND PROBLEMS

Spider mites, scale insects and brown tips on leaves can occur in dry, centrally heated air.

CARE

Keep soil evenly moist, but water less in winter. Feed weekly with diluted liquid fertilizer in spring and summer, and as long as leaves are being produced. Mist or wipe leaves with a damp cloth or sponge to provide humidity.

MEDIA

Use all-purpose potting mix. Hydroculture is easier as it requires less frequent watering and repotting.

OVERALL RATING   5.3

Removal of chemical vapours

Ease of growth and maintenance

Resistance to insect infestation

Transpiration rate

POINSETTIA
(Euphorbia pulcherrima)

Poinsettia, with its brilliant red bracts, immediately evokes the atmosphere of the Christmas season. Seen in homes, businesses, shopping centres and churches, it is one of the most popular winter holiday plants.

Poinsettia's flowers are insignificant. It is the plant's highly decorative bracts (leaves) that account for its appeal. Its lower bracts are green and the upper bracts are red, white, pink, speckled or marbled.

The poinsettia was first discovered growing wild in southern Mexico and introduced as a houseplant by Joel Poinsett in 1830. Albert Ecke first grew poinsettias commercially in the early 1900s. His son, Paul, assumed the business and began to develop sturdier varieties. It is estimated that 90 per cent of all poinsettias in the world originated from the Paul Ecke Ranch in California.

FAMILY
Euphorbiaceae (spurge).

ORIGIN
Southern Mexico.

LIGHT
Semi-shade.

TEMPERATURE
Day: 18–21°C (65–70°F); night: 10–18°C (50–65°F).

PESTS AND PROBLEMS
Rarely white flies. Root rot may occur if the soil is too moist.

CARE
Water thoroughly when the top layer of soil is dry. Water less during its rest period from spring to mid summer. Apply weak fertilizer every two weeks during period of active growth.

MEDIA
Use an all-purpose potting mix. It can also be grown in hydroculture.

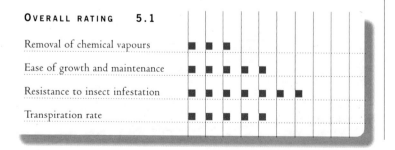

OVERALL RATING   **5.1**

Removal of chemical vapours

Ease of growth and maintenance

Resistance to insect infestation

Transpiration rate

DWARF AZALEA

(*Rhododendron simsii* "Compacta")

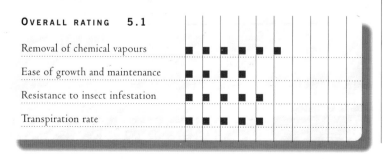

Nurseries in Belgium were the first to introduce azaleas as a seasonal indoor plant around 1850. Today they remain extremely popular as more varieties and colours come on the market.

This dwarf variety of azalea is also commonly referred to as florist's azalea. It is generally regarded as an indoor plant but can survive outdoors if protected from frost. For a breath of spring in the winter, this plant is hard to beat. Commercial breeding has produced plants that flower from winter to spring. They are sold as seasonal flowering plants, but can be purchased nearly all year round. Azalea is not a "throw away" plant. Trim off dead blooms and leaves, replant in a slightly larger pot, and move to a shady spot outdoors in late spring.

When purchasing azaleas, do not select one that is in full bloom. Rather, choose one whose buds are still set but showing some colour. This ensures that you will have the benefit of a long flowering period.

FAMILY

Ericaceae (heath).

ORIGIN

Central China and Japan.

LIGHT

Semi-shade.

TEMPERATURE

Day: 13–20°C (55–68°F); night: 7–16°C (45–60°F).

PESTS AND PROBLEMS

Spider mites in too warm and dry a location.

CARE

Keep soil moist with room-temperature soft water or rainwater. Do not begin feeding until six weeks after blooming has finished. Then feed every 14 days with all-purpose fertilizer. In autumn, use a fertilizer that is higher in phosphorus than nitrogen to encourage strong blooms. Mist only when not in bloom.

MEDIA

Azaleas prefer an acid soil. Use commercial azalea mix or equal parts potting mix, peat moss and sand.

OVERALL RATING   5.1

Removal of chemical vapours		
Ease of growth and maintenance		
Resistance to insect infestation		
Transpiration rate		

PEACOCK PLANT

(Calathea makoyana)

Grown for its unique foliage, the peacock plant is sometime confused with its close relative the prayer plant. However, it has its own distinctive markings.

C. makoyana obtained its common name from the exquisite markings on its leaves that somewhat resemble a peacock's tail. It features 25 to 30-cm (10 – 12-in) long oval leaves that have mid-green edges and a silvery background with dark-green blotches.

The peacock plant can be difficult to grow in the home. Variations in temperature, humidity and moisture may cause the leaves to roll up and turn brown.

However, the varieties currently available have been bred through tissue culturing of the strongest plants. As a result, it is now a tougher plant that can better withstand the rigours of the home environment. Its highly decorative foliage makes the extra effort needed to maintain it worthwhile.

FAMILY

Marantaceae (arrowroot).

ORIGIN

Tropical regions of the Americas.

LIGHT

Semi-shade.

TEMPERATURE

18–27°C (65–80°F).

PESTS AND PROBLEMS

Spider mites and scale insects.

CARE

Keep the soil evenly moist (not soggy) with room-temperature water. Feed every two weeks with a dilute liquid fertilizer in spring and summer. Mist often.

MEDIA

Performs well in standard commercial potting mix. In hydroculture, the pebbles should occasionally be flushed with fresh water, because it is sensitive to the build-up of salts.

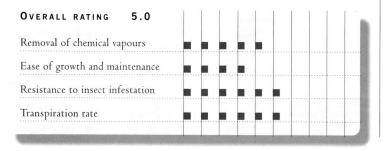

OVERALL RATING	5.0
Removal of chemical vapours	
Ease of growth and maintenance	
Resistance to insect infestation	
Transpiration rate	

ALOE VERA

(Aloe barbadensis)

Aloe vera is also known as the medicinal plant. An important herb, it has been widely used in folk medicine for over 3,000 years, both as a liniment for treating burns and as a drink for treating arthritis. Aloe is a popular base for many cosmetics and is found in hundreds of products on the market today.

Aloe is a succulent that grows in clustering rosettes of stiff, upright leaves. The foliage is usually light green with white spots. The whole leaf turns grey as it matures. All species of aloe bloom only after reaching maturity. It is easily propagated by transplanting its numerous offsets.

Like the snake plant, orchids and bromeliads, aloe differs from most houseplants in that it releases oxygen and absorbs carbon dioxide at night, and for this reason should be considered for the bedroom.

FAMILY

Liliaceae (lily).

ORIGIN

South Africa.

LIGHT

Full sun to semi-sun.

TEMPERATURE

18–24°C (65–75°F); winter nights 4°C (40°F) minimum.

PESTS AND PROBLEMS

Rarely attacked by pests.

CARE

Water moderately in spring, summer and autumn; water sparingly in winter. Feed once a month in spring and summer. Do not feed in autumn and winter.

MEDIA

Use a standard commercial potting mix that drains well.

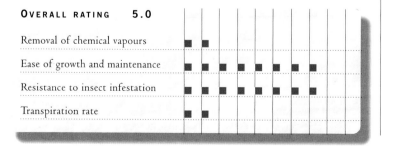

OVERALL RATING   5.0

Removal of chemical vapours	
Ease of growth and maintenance	
Resistance to insect infestation	
Transpiration rate	

CYCLAMEN

(Cyclamen persicum)

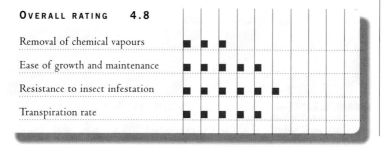

Cyclamen has been a popular seasonal flowering plant since about 1900. There are approximately 15 species in the genus. However, *C. persicum* is the species most often sold in florists as an indoor plant. It is valued for its blooms that rise up on stems from a bed of heart-shaped, dark green or marbled leaves. Cyclamen originates in mountainous forest regions. Therefore, it prefers a cool location with good air circulation. They often last much longer in a cool bedroom than in a warm living room and should never be placed near a heat source. Miniature varieties seem to be more long-lasting.

The flowering season lasts from September to April. Its flowers, which resemble shooting stars, are available in white, pink, red, salmon or violet. With proper environmental conditions, flowers may last several weeks. It is best to purchase plants whose buds are already showing colour. Most people discard the plants once blooming has ceased, but with care they can be kept.

FAMILY

Primulaceae (primrose).

ORIGIN

Eastern Mediterranean.

LIGHT

Semi-shade.

TEMPERATURE

16–22°C (60–72°F).

PESTS AND PROBLEMS

Spider mites and cyclamen mites.

CARE

Cyclamen need careful watering. Keep the soil moist from autumn until spring. In summer when the plant is at rest, keep the soil only slightly damp. Feed with half-strength "African violet" formula every two weeks when in bloom.

MEDIA

Performs best in commercial potting mix labelled "African violet mix".

OVERALL RATING   4.8

Removal of chemical vapours	■ ■ ■
Ease of growth and maintenance	■ ■ ■ ■
Resistance to insect infestation	■ ■ ■ ■ ■
Transpiration rate	■ ■ ■ ■

URN PLANT

(Aechmea fasciata)

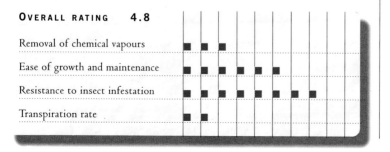

The urn plant belongs to the bromeliad family, which are strikingly handsome plants that are sought for their brightly coloured bracts. However, their rosettes often are of interest in their own right. These plants are long-lasting and have gained in popularity in recent years.

The urn plant consists of tough, coarse leaves that are blotched silver and sea-green and edged with prickly spines. These leaves overlap into a rosette that forms a watertight urn or vase, hence its common name. A plant may take up to five years to send forth a bluish bract that turns pink as it matures. This bract will last for several weeks, but each plant blooms only once. For additional blooms, repot the offsets and allow to mature.

In their native jungle habitat, urn plants grow lodged in branches of trees or on rocks. A gardener can recreate the setting by wiring the plant to a tree branch and packing sphagnum moss around it. Indoors it is probably best to grow them in soil. In its natural surroundings, the vase or urn allows the plant to survive between rain showers. A plant grown in soil does not need water in its vase.

FAMILY
Bromeliaceae (pineapple).

ORIGIN
Brazil.

LIGHT
Semi-sun.

TEMPERATURE
16–21°C (60–70°F).

PESTS AND PROBLEMS
This plant is highly resistant to pests, although under extreme conditions, it may be attacked by mealybugs.

CARE
Provide half-strength liquid fertilizer to the soil (not the urn) in spring and summer. Keep the root ball damp, but allow the top soil to dry slightly between waterings.

MEDIA
Grows best in a commercial potting mix for epiphytic plants. Hydroculture is a less satisfactory alternative.

OVERALL RATING   **4.8**

Removal of chemical vapours

Ease of growth and maintenance

Resistance to insect infestation

Transpiration rate

TULIP

(*Tulipa gesneriana*)

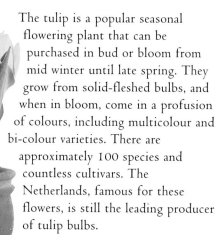

The tulip is a popular seasonal flowering plant that can be purchased in bud or bloom from mid winter until late spring. They grow from solid-fleshed bulbs, and when in bloom, come in a profusion of colours, including multicolour and bi-colour varieties. There are approximately 100 species and countless cultivars. The Netherlands, famous for these flowers, is still the leading producer of tulip bulbs.

For the home grower, it is easiest to buy pre-planted containers of bulbs that have been cooled to start the forcing process. If the bulbs have not been cooled, it may be necessary to store the bulbs in the vegetable compartment of a refrigerator for at least six weeks prior to potting in soil. After flowering, continue to provide moisture and sunlight to maintain the foliage. When the weather warms, place the pots outside.

Although tulips are seasonal indoor plants, they are nevertheless good for cleaning the air. They have been shown to remove formaldehyde, xylene and ammonia from the atmosphere.

FAMILY
Liliaceae (lily).

ORIGIN
Southeastern Europe and central Asia.

LIGHT
Full sun to semi-sun.

TEMPERATURE
13–21°C (55–70°F).

PESTS AND PROBLEMS
Aphids.

CARE
Keep the soil evenly moist. Never allow to dry out.

MEDIA
Use an all-purpose potting mix or mix equal parts of soil, sand and peat moss.

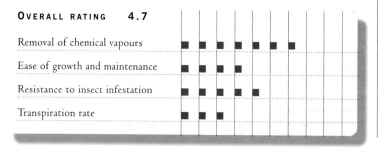

OVERALL RATING   4.7

Removal of chemical vapours

Ease of growth and maintenance

Resistance to insect infestation

Transpiration rate

MOTH ORCHID

(*Phalenopsis* sp.)

The moth orchid's exotic blooms provide a breath of spring in the dead of winter. They can even be induced to bloom all year round. For the first time orchid-grower, the moth orchid should be first on the list. It is more forgiving of the typical indoor environment than others. This orchid has proved to be quite effective in removing xylene from the atmosphere.

The *Phalenopsis* orchid is monopodial. This means that it grows upwards on a single stem by producing new leaves at the top of the plant. It usually blooms from winter to spring. It produces 5 to 7.6-cm (2 – 3-in) flowers of white, yellow, pink, red, violet, brown, or green, or multicoloured. Its common name is inspired by the moth-like appearance of the flowers. Its leaves are thick, broad and leathery.

After flowering, cut the stalk just below the node that produced the first flower. With proper conditions, the stem will branch and produce more flowers. In this way, the plant can be encouraged to bloom almost all year long. Hybrids, which are bred to suit the environmental conditions typically found in the home, are the best choice.

FAMILY

Orchidaceae (orchid).

ORIGIN

Eastern India, Southeast Asia, Indonesia, Philippines, northern Australia, New Guinea.

LIGHT

Semi-shade.

TEMPERATURE

Day: 21–27°C (70–80°F); night: 16–18°C (60–65°F).

PESTS AND PROBLEMS

Overwatering can cause fungal infections. Attacks of scale insects and spider mites may occur in air that is too dry.

CARE

A soak-and-dry cycle is best. Feed every two weeks during growing season with diluted liquid fertilizer. Mist often.

MEDIA

Use a commercially prepared orchid mix or decayed oak leaves, Spanish moss or sphagnum moss. It can also grow in hydroculture.

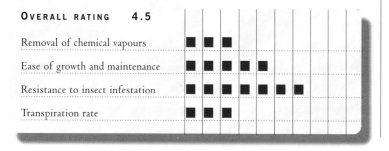

OVERALL RATING	4.5									
Removal of chemical vapours	■	■	■							
Ease of growth and maintenance	■	■	■	■						
Resistance to insect infestation	■	■	■	■	■	■	■			
Transpiration rate	■	■	■							

KALANCHOE

(Kalanchoe blossfeldiana)

Kalanchoe is a favourite among seasonal flowering plants, although it is available through the year. It produces beautiful flowers in an abundance of colours and is quite easy to grow and maintain.

Its stunning array of flowers appear at the end of thin stems protruding upwards through shiny green, oval leaves. Growers have developed colours ranging from reds, yellows, and apricot, through orange, pink, and violet.

Although the kalanchoe is relatively poor for removing indoor air toxins or adding much needed moisture to dry winter air, it is exceptionally beautiful when in bloom. After blooming, cut off flower stems and do not water until new growth begins. It will probably do better outdoors in summer.

FAMILY

Crassulaceae (orpine).

ORIGIN

Madagascar.

LIGHT

Full sun.

TEMPERATURE

16–26°C (60–78°F).

PESTS AND PROBLEMS

Aphids and mealybugs, especially on leaf undersides.

CARE

From March to August, feed every two weeks with a fertilizer formulated for flowering plants. To bloom in winter, the kalanchoe must rest in autumn. Water moderately in summer, but keep nearly dry in winter.

MEDIA

Can be grown in soil, soil-less media or hydroculture.

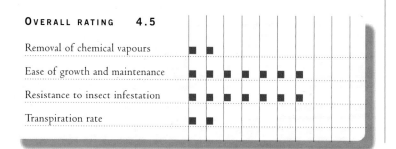

OVERALL RATING	4.5								
Removal of chemical vapours	■	■							
Ease of growth and maintenance	■	■	■	■	■	■	■		
Resistance to insect infestation	■	■	■	■	■	■			
Transpiration rate	■	■							

Index

Aechmea fasciata 23, 34, 132–3

Aglaonema crispum 'Silver Queen' 23, 33, 116–17

air: indoor pollution 7, 8–13
    purification through use of plants 18–19, 21–29

air purification systems 28–29

airplane plant *see* spider plant

allergy 11–12

Aloe barbadensis 23, 32, 128–9

aloe vera 23, 32, 128–9

anthurium (Lady Jane) 23, 24, 32, 118–9

Anthurium andraeanum 23, 32, 118–9

Araucaria heterophylla 23, 32, 33, 100–1

areca palm 23, 24, 32, 35, 40–1

arrowhead vine 23, 24, 32, 33, 76–7

Associated Landscape Contractors of America (ALCA) 21

azalea, dwarf 23, 24, 33, 124–5

bamboo palm 23, 32, 44–5

banana, dwarf 23, 32, 104–5

begonia, wax 23, 32, 86–7

Begonia semperflorens 23, 32, 86–7

bioeffluents, removal from air 11, 25–6

biohome 21–22

Boston fern 23, 32, 33, 56–7

Brassaia actinophylla 23, 33, 84–5

breathing zones, personal 26, 28

butterfly palm *see* areca palm

cactus: Christmas 23, 32, 106–7
    Easter 23, 32, 106–7

Calathea makoyana 23, 24, 33, 126–7

Chamaedorea elegans 23, 24, 32, 33, 80–1
    C. seifrizii 23, 33, 44–5

chemicals, volatile 9–13, 18, 21–5
    removal rates by houseplants 23–5

Chinese evergreen 23, 33, 116–17

Chlorophytum comosum 'Vittatum' 23, 32, 33, 114–15

Christmas cactus 23, 32, 106–7

Chrysalidocarpus lutescens 23, 24, 32, 35, 40–1

Chrysanthemum morifolium 23, 24, 32, 66–7

Cissus rhombifolia 'Ellen Danika' 23, 32, 33, 108-9

Codiaeum variegatum pictum 23, 32, 33, 120–1

containers 36–7

corn plant 23, 24, 33, 60–1

cot death 12–13

croton 23, 32, 33, 120–1

cyclamen 23, 33, 130–1

Cyclamen persicum 23, 33, 130–1

daisy, gerbera 23, 32, 68–9

date palm, dwarf 23, 24, 32, 52–3

dendrobium orchid 23, 24, 32, 112–13

Dendrobium sp. 23, 24, 32, 112–13

Dieffenbachia camilla 23, 24, 32, 33, 94–5
    D. 'Exotica Compacta' 23, 24, 32, 32, 78–9

dracaena
    'Janet Craig' 23, 33, 48–9
    'Warneckei' 23, 24, 33, 70–1

Dracaena deremensis 'Compacta' 48, 70
    D. d. 'Janet Craig' 23, 33, 48–9
    D. d. 'Warneckei' 23, 24, 33, 70–1
    D. fragrans 'Massangeana' 23, 24, 33, 60–1
    D. marginata 23, 24, 32, 72–3
    D. m. 'Tricolor' 72–3

dragon tree 23, 24, 33, 72–3

dumb cane 23, 24, 32, 33, 78–9, 94–5

dwarf azalea 23, 24, 33, 124–5

dwarf banana 23, 32, 104–5

dwarf date palm 23, 24, 32, 52–3

Easter cactus 23, 32, 106–7

ecosystems: of a building 28
    plants of 15–19

elephant ear philodendron 23, 33, 96–7

English ivy 23, 32, 33, 50–1

Environmental Protection Agency (EPA) 8, 11

Epipremnum aureum 23, 33, 62–3

Euphorbia pulcherrima 23, 33, 122–3

fern: Boston 23, 32, 33, 56–7
    Kimberley queen 23, 24, 32, 33, 64–5

ficus alii 23, 32, 54–5

Ficus benjamina 23, 24, 32, 54, 82–3
    F. elastica see F. robusta
    F. macleilandii 'Alii' 23, 32, 54–5
    F. robusta 23, 32, 33, 46–7

fig, weeping 23, 24, 32, 82–3

florist's mum 23, 24, 32, 66–7

formaldehyde 10, 21, 23–5

gases, toxic 10–13, 18–19, 21–5, 28

gerbera daisy 23, 32, 68–9

Gerbera jamesonii 23, 32, 68–9

golden pothos 23, 33, 62–3

goosehead plant *see* syngonium

heart-leaf philodendron 23, 33, 90–1

Hedera helix 23, 32, 32, 50–1

Homalomena wallisii 23, 24, 33, 100–1

houseplants
    biological functions 16–19, 27
    care 30–7
    most eco-friendly 40–139
    role in air purification 18–19, 21–29

humidity 9, 18, 28, 30–1

hydroponics/hydroculture 34–5

indoor air quality (IAQ) 7, 9–13, 21–29

ivy: English 23, 32, 33, 50–1
    oakleaf 23, 32, 33, 108–9

Janet Craig (dracaena) 23, 33, 48–9

Joseph's Coat *see* croton

kalanchoe 23, 32, 138–9

Kalanchoe blossfeldiana 23, 32, 138–9

Kimberley queen 23, 24, 32, 33, 64–5

king of hearts 23, 24, 33, 100–1

lacy tree philodendron 23, 33, 78–9

Lady Jane (anthurium) 23, 24, 32, 118

lady palm 23, 24, 25, 32, 35, 42–3

legionnaire's disease 9, 11

light, plants' requirements 31–4

lily, peace 23, 24, 25, 32, 33, 58–9

lily turf 23, 24, 32, 33, 110–11

Liriope spicata 23, 24, 32, 33, 110–11

Maranta leuconeura 'Kerchoveana' 23, 33, 102–3

microbes, plant-root 18–19, 25, 26, 27, 28

moth orchid 23, 24, 33, 136–7

'mother-in-law's tongue' *see* snake plant

mould spores in air 25–6

Musa cavendishii 23, 32, 104–5

multiple chemical sensitivity (MCS) 12

National Aeronautics and Space
Administrator (NASA) 7, 21–23, 68, 114
Neanthe bella see Parlour palm
Nephrolepis exaltata 'Bostoniensis' 23, 32,
    33, 56–7
    N. obliterata 23, 24, 32, 33, 64–5
Norfolk Island pine 23, 32, 33, 98–9

oakleaf ivy 23, 32, 33, 108–9
off-gassing 13, 28
orchid: dendrobium 23, 24, 32, 112–13
    moth 23, 24, 33, 136–7

palm: areca 23, 24, 32, 35, 40–1
    bamboo 23, 32, 44–5
    dwarf date 23, 24, 32, 52–3
    lady 23, 24, 25, 32, 35, 42–3
    parlour 23, 24, 32, 33, 80–1
parlour palm 23, 24, 32, 33, 80–1
peace lily 23, 24, 25, 32, 33, 58–9
peacock plant 23, 24, 33, 126–7
pests 37
Phalenopsis sp. 23, 24, 33, 136–7
philodendron: elephant ear 23, 33, 96–7
    heart-leaf 23, 33, 90–1
    lacy tree 23, 33, 78–9
    red emerald 23, 33, 74–5
    spade-leaf *see* philodendron, elephant ear
Philodendron bastatum see P. domesticum
    P. domesticum 23, 33, 96–7
    P. erubescens 23, 33, 74–5
    P. oxycardium 23, 33, 90–1
    P. scandens see P. oxycardium
    P. selloum 23, 33, 78–9
    P. tuxla see P. domesticum
Phoenix roebelenii 23, 24, 32, 52–3
photosynthesis 15, 16, 17
phytochemicals 19
pine, Norfolk Island 23, 32, 33, 98–9
poinsettia 23, 33, 122–3
pollution: indoor air 7, 8–13
    reducing through use of plants 18–19,
    21–29
pothos, golden 23, 33, 62–3
prayer plant 23, 33, 102–3

red emerald philodendron 23, 33, 74–5
Rhapis excelsa 23, 24, 25, 32, 35, 42–3
rhizosphere 16, 18–19
Rhododendron simsii 'Compacta' 23, 24, 33,
    124–5
rubber plant 23, 34, 33, 46–7

Sansevieria trifasciata 23, 32, 33, 92–3
schefflera 23, 33, 84–5
Schlumbergera bridgesii 23, 32, 106–7
    S. rhipsalidopsis 23, 35, 106–7
sick building syndrome (SBS) 7, 11–13,
    21, 22
snake plant 23, 32, 33, 92–3
spade-leaf philodendron *see* elephant ear
philodendron
Spathiphyllum sp 23, 24, 25, 32, 33, 58–9
spider plant 23, 32, 33, 114–15
stomata 17, 27
sub-irrigation 36–7
sudden infant death syndrome (SIDS)
    12–13
syngonium (arrowhead vine) 23, 24, 32,
    33, 76–7
Syngonium podophyllum 23, 24, 32, 33, 76–7

toxins, removal from air by plants 18–19,
    21–5, 28
translocation 18
transpiration 16–18, 26, 27
tulip 23, 24, 32, 134–135
Tulipa gesneriana 23, 24, 32, 33, 134–5
turf, lily 23, 24, 32, 33, 110–11

umbrella tree *see* schefflera
urn plant 23, 24, 32, 33, 132–3

vapour, water 18, 27
vapours, chemical *see* volatile organic
chemicals
vine, arrowhead 23, 24, 32, 33, 76–7
volatile organic chemicals (VOCs) 10–13,
    18, 21–5

Warneckei 23, 24, 33, 68–9
wastewater, utilizing 28–9
watering 36; *see also* hydroponics *and* sub-
irrigation
water vapour 18, 27
wax begonia 23, 32, 84–5
weeping fig 23, 24, 32, 80–1
white butterfly plant *see* syngonium

yellow palm *see* areca palm

Abbreviations

ALCA – Associated Landscape
Contractors of America
ASHRAE – American Society of
Heating, Refrigeration and Air
Conditioning Engineers
BRI – Building-related illness
CO$_2$ – carbon dioxide
CRI – Carpet and Rug Institute
DNA – Deoryribonucleic acid
EPA – Environmental Protection Agency
HVAC – Heating, ventilation and air
conditioning
IAQ – Indoor air quality
IPM – Integrated pest management
MCS – Multiple chemical sensitivity
NASA – National Aeronautics and Space
Administration
NIOSH – National Institute for
Occupational Safety and Health
PCAC – Plants for Clean Air Council
SAD – Seasonal affective disorder
SBR – Styrene butadiene rubber
SBS – Sick building syndrome
SIDS – Sudden infant death syndrome
VOCs – Volatile organic chemicals

Glossary

Absorption The passing of chemicals or other substances into plant tissue.

Adsorption The adhesion of a gas, liquid or dissolved substance to a surface.

Aerobic Requiring oxygen for growth.

Allergen Substance that induces allergy.

Allergy Hypersensitivity; the harmful reaction of antibody to its specific antigen.

Anaerobic Growing in the absence of oxygen.

Antibodies Specific molecules formed in the body in response to the presence of an antigen. Once formed, future exposure to that particular antigen creates an allergic response.

Antigen Substance that induces a specific allergic or immune response.

Bioeffluents Chemicals released during human respiration.

Biosphere The zone around the earth where life naturally occurs, extending from the deep crust to the lower atmosphere.

Bract A modified leaf shaped like a leaf or flower petal. Bracts are often highly coloured, as in the poinsettia, and may support a less showy flower.

Bromeliad A member of the Bromeliaceae family. Bromeliads are epiphytic plants and can be grown supported on tree bark and other non-soil surfaces.

Chlorophyll The green pigment in plant leaves essential to the process of photosynthesis.

Cultivar A term for a plant that has been bred in cultivation and that differs from the typical wild species.

Dormant period A rest period in which a plant ceases to grow, usually during the winter months.

Epiphyte A plant that grows on another plant but that is not a parasite. It produces its own food by photosynthesis. Such plants are also known as "air plants".

Expanded clay aggregate A lightweight, highly porous aggregate obtained by heating selected clays at temperatures from $816 - 1093°C$ ($1500 - 2000°F$). Its porous nature allows for maximum air and water exchange in hydroculture.

Foliage plant A plant that is grown indoors primarily for the display of its leaves. Although some foliage plants bloom, their flowers are usually insignificant.

Humidity The amount of water vapour in the air.

Hydroculture The hydroponic technique of growing houseplants in a water-tight container with support substrate other than soil (for example, expanded clay aggregate), and supplied with a nutrient solution.

Hydroponics The technique of growing plants in a medium other than soil whereby water and nutrients flow past plant roots; primarily used in commercial food production.

Hypersensitivity Increased sensitivity or allergy, to certain substances.

Immunoglobulins (**Ig**) Alternative name for antibodies.

Inert Not active.

Isoprenoids Naturally occurring materials such as terpenes and rubber produced by plants.

Microbe A microscopic organism.

Microorganisms Microbes; minute forms of life, individually too small to be seen without the aid of a microscope.

Off-gas To give off or to emit.

Personal breathing zone An area, approximately $0.17 - 0.23$ cu. m ($6 - 8$ cu. ft) encompassing an individual.

Phloem The tissue system in plants that conducts food, principally sugars, downwards from leaves into stems and roots.

Photosynthesis The manufacture of carbohydrate foods (sugars) from carbon dioxide and water in the presence of light and chlorophyll.

Phytochemical A chemical manufactured by a plant.

Relative humidity The amount of water vapour the air is holding expressed as a percentage of the maximum amount the air could potentially hold at that temperature.

Repot To transfer a plant to a new container or renew the soil in the pot to revitalize plant growth.

Respiration The oxidation of foods (sugars) within a living organism to release stored energy, making it available for growth and other uses.

Rhizosphere Area around plants influenced by substances excreted by plant roots.

Stomata Microscopic openings on plant leaves that allow water vapour, oxygen and other gases to pass in or out of the leaf.

Sub-irrigation The technique of growing plants in soil filled, water-tight containers in which water is introduced below the soil surface.

Symbiotic A relationship of mutual benefit or dependence.

Systemic activity The ability of a plant to absorb and translocate certain chemicals.

Terpenes Complex, unsaturated hydrocarbons found in resins; an essential oil derived from pine trees and other plants.

Translocation The transport of food materials and other organic substances through tissue systems from one part of a plant to another.

Transpiration The natural process of water evaporation from plant leaves. Transpiration produces cooling and air movement around plant leaves.

Ventilation Dilution of stale indoor air with fresh outside air.

Xylem The tissue system in plants that conducts water and dissolved minerals upward from roots to stems and leaves.

Bibliography

All About Houseplants, Ortho Books (Chevron Chemical Co.), San Francisco, 1982.

Davidson, William, *The Houseplant Survival Manual*, Hamlyn Publishing Group Ltd, London, 1984.

Giese, M., U. Bauer-Doranth, C. Langebartels, and H. Sandermann, Jr., "Detoxification of Formaldehyde by the Spider Plant (*Chlorophytum comosum* L.) and by soybean (*Glycine max* L.) cell suspension cultures," *Plant Physiology*, 1994, 104: 1301–1309

Green, G. H., "The Health Implications of the Level of Indoor Air Humidity". Proceedings of the Third International Conference of Indoor Air Quality and Climate. Vol. I. *Recent Advances in the Health Sciences and Technology*, 1984, 71-78.

Greenfield, Ellen J., *House Dangerous*, Vintage Books, New York, 1987.

Griffin, Katherine, "When Your Office Calls in Sick So Will You", *Health*, January/February 1993, 79-82.

Hall, Stephen, "Allergic to the 20th Century", *Health*, May/June 1993, 73-85.

Hammer, Nelson, *Interior Landscape Design*, McGraw-Hill, Inc., New York, 1992.

Heitz, Halina, *Indoor Plants* Hauppauge, Barron's Educational Series, Inc., New York, 1991.

"Look After Your Greens", *The Guardian*, December 14, 1995.

McDonald, Elvin, *The New Houseplant*, Macmillan Publishing Company, New York, 1993.

Menzies, R., et al., "The Effect of Varying Levels of Outdoor-Air Supply on the Symptoms of Sick Building Syndrome", *New England Journal of Medicine*, (1993) 328(12), 821-826.

"Need an Air Freshener? Try Plants", *The New York Times*, February 13, 1994.

"Plants May Play Bigger Role in Cleaning Air", *The New York Times*, August 27, 1995.

Reinikainen, L. M., et al., "The Effect of Air Humidification on Different Symptoms in Office Workers. An Epidemiologic Study", *Environ. Int.*, 1991, 17: 243-250.

Reinikainen, L. M., et al. "The Effect of Air Humidification on Symptoms and Perception of Indoor Air Quality. A Six-Period Cross-over Trial." *Arch. Environ. Health*, 1992, 47: 8-15.

Relf, Diane. (Ed.), *The Role of Horticulture in Human Well-Being and Social Development*, Timber Press, Inc., Portland, Oregon, 1992.

Rovira, A. D., "Root Excretions in Relation to the Rhizosphere Effect. IV. Influence of Plant Species, Age of Plant, Light, Temperature and Calcium Nutrition on Exudation", *Plant Soil*, 1959, 53-64.

Rovira, A. D., "Interactions Between Plant Roots and Soil Microorganisms", *Annual Review of Microbiology*, 1965, 19: 241-266.

Rovira, A. D., "Plant Root Exudates and Their Influence Upon Soil Microorganisms", K. W. Baker and W. C. Snyder (eds.) *Ecology of Soil-born Plant Pathogens*, University of California Press, 1970, 170-182.

Rovira, A. C. and C. B. Davey, "Biology of the Rhizosphere", E. W. Carson (ed.) *The Plant Root and Its Environment*, University Press of Virginia, 1974, 153-204.

Samet, J. M. and John D. Spengler (eds.), *Indoor Air Pollution a Health Perspective* John Hopkins University Press, Baltimore, 1991.

Snyder, Stuart D., *Building Interiors, Plants and Automation*, Englewood Cliffs, Prentice Hall, New Jersey, 1990.

Soviero, Marcelle, "Can Your House Make You Sick?" *Popular Science*, July 1992.

Steinman, David, "The Architecture of Illness", *Vegetarian Times*, January 1993.

Sunset Houseplants A to Z, Lane Publishing Co., Menlo Park, California, 1989.

Tukey, Jr., H. B., "The Leaching of Substances From Plants", *Annual Review Plant Physiology*, 1970, 21: 305-324.

US Environmental Protection Agency Report to Congress, *Indoor Air Quality in Public Buildings:* Vols. I and II (1988) EPA/00/6-88/009ab.

US Environmental Protection Agency Report to Congress, *Indoor Air Quality: Executive Summary and Recommendations* (1989) EPA/400/I-89/001A.

US Environmental Protection Agency Report to Congress, *Indoor Air Quality: Assessment and Control of Indoor Air Pollution* (1989) EPA/400/I-89/001C.

Wallace, L. A., et al., "The Influence of Personal Activities on Exposure to Volatile Organic Compounds", *Environmental Research*, 1990 50: 37-55.

Wallace, L. A., et al., "Personal Exposure to Volatile Organic Compounds, I:

Direct Measurement in Breathing-Zone Air, Food and Exhaled Breath", *Environmental Research*, 1984, 35: 293-319.

Wang, T. C., "A Study of Bioeffluents in a College Classroom", *ASHRAE Trans.*, 1975, 81(Pt. I): 32-44.

Wolverton, B. C., "Higher Plants for Recycling Human Waste into Food, Potable Water and Revitalized Air in a Closed Life Support System", NASA Research Report No. 192, August 1980.

Wolverton, B. C., R. C. McDonald and E. A. Watkins, Jr., "Foliage Plants for Removing Indoor Air Pollutants from Energy-Efficient Homes", *Economic Botany*, 1984, 38(2): 224-228.

Wolverton, B. C., R. C. McDonald and H. H. Mesick, "Foliage Plants for the Indoor Removal of the Primary Combustion Gases Carbon Monoxide and Nitrogen Oxides", *Journal of the Mississippi Academy of Sciences*, 1985, 30: 1-8.

Wolverton, B. C., "Natural Systems for Wastewater Treatment and Water Reuse for Space and Earthly Applications", Implementing Water Reuse, Proceedings of Water Reuse Symposium IV, Denver, Colorado, August 1987.

Wolverton, B. C. A. Johnson and K. Bounds, "Interior Landscape Plants for Indoor Air Pollution Abatement", NASA/ALCA Final Report, *Plants for Clean Air Council*, Mitchellville, Maryland, 1989.

Wolverton, B. C., "Plants and Their Microbial Assistants, Nature's Answer to Earth's Environmental Pollution Problems", Biological Life Support Technologies: Commercial Opportunities, M. Nelson and G. Soffen (eds.), proceedings from a workshop sponsored by NASA, 1989.

Wolverton, B. C., Rebecca McCaleb and W. L. Douglas, "Bioregenerative Space and Terrestrial Habitat", Ninth Biennial Princeton Conference on Space Manufacturing, Space Studies Institute, Princeton, New Jersey (May 11, 1989).

Wolverton, B. C. and J. Wolverton, "Removal of Formaldehyde From Sealed Chambers by Azalea, Poinsettia and Dieffenbachia", Research Report No. WES/100/01-91/005, *Plants for Clean Air Council*, Mitchellville, Maryland, 1991.

Wolverton, B. C. and J. Wolverton "Bioregenerative Life Support Systems for Energy-Efficient Buildings", Proceedings of International Conference of Life Support and Biospherics, Huntsville, Alabama, 1992.

Wolverton, B. C. and J. D. Wolverton "Plants and Soil Microorganisms — Removal of Formaldehyde, Xylene and Ammonia From the Indoor Environment", *Journal of the Mississippi Academy of Sciences*, 1993, 38(2): 11-15.

Wolverton, B. C. and J. D. Wolverton, "Interior Plants: Their Influence on Airborne Microbes Inside Energy-Efficient Buildings", *Journal of the Mississippi Academy of Sciences*, 1996, 41(2): 99-105.

Wolverton, J. and B. C. Wolverton, "Improving Indoor Air Quality Using Orchids and Bromeliads", Research Report No. WES/100/12-91/006. *Plants for Clean Air Council*, Mitchellville, Maryland, 1991.